I0824532

ARCHITECTURE AGAINST ARCHITECTURE

ARCHITECTURE AGAINST ARCHITECTURE

A Manifesto

Reinier de Graaf

VERSO
London • New York

First published by Verso 2026

The manufacturer's authorized representative in the EU for product safety (GPSR) is LOGOS EUROPE, 9 rue Nicolas Poussin, 17000, La Rochelle, France
Contact@logoseurope.eu

1 3 5 7 9 10 8 6 4 2

Verso
UK: 6 Meard Street, London W1F 0EG
US: 207 East 32nd Street, New York, NY 10016
versobooks.com

Verso is the imprint of New Left Books

ISBN-13: 978-1-80429-903-6
ISBN-13: 978-1-80429-906-7 (US EBK)
ISBN-13: 978-1-80429-905-0 (UK EBK)

British Library Cataloguing in Publication Data
A catalogue record for this book is available from the British Library

Library of Congress Cataloging-in-Publication Data

Names: Graaf, Reinier de, 1964- author
Title: Architecture against architecture : a manifesto / Reinier de Graaf.
Description: London : Verso, 2026. | Includes bibliographical references.
Identifiers: LCCN 2025043996 (print) | LCCN 2025043997 (ebook) | ISBN 9781804299036 hardback | ISBN 9781804299067 ebook
Subjects: LCSH: Architectural practice | Architecture
Classification: LCC NA1995 .G685 2026 (print) | LCC NA1995 (ebook)
LC record available at https://lccn.loc.gov/2025043996
LC ebook record available at https://lccn.loc.gov/2025043997

Typeset in Garamond by Biblichor Ltd, Scotland
Printed and bound by CPI Group (UK) Ltd, Croydon CR0 4YY

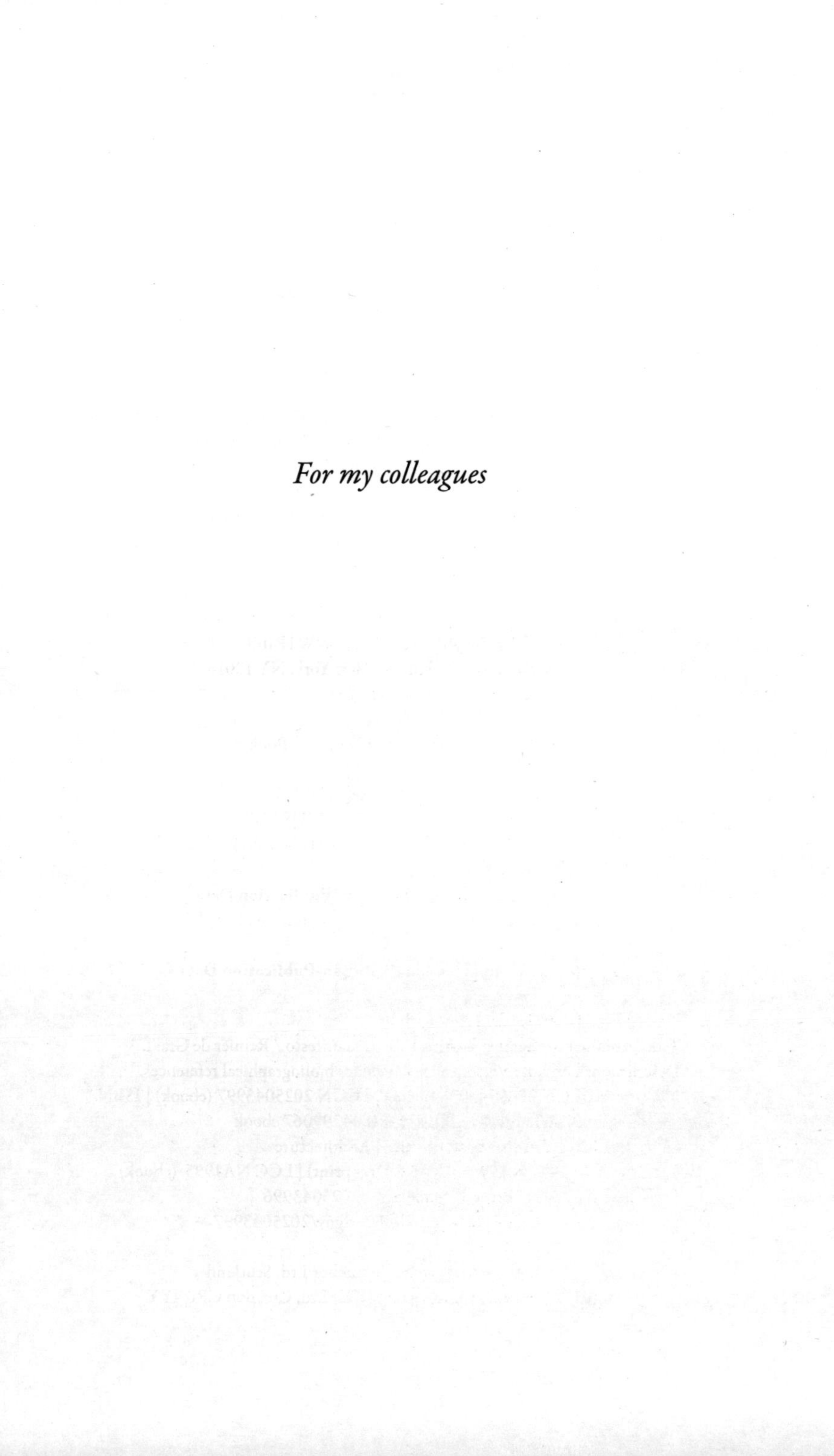

For my colleagues

Contents

Preface

What should we do? It is the most frequently asked question I get in relation to my books, usually once the official part of the events at which they are being debated is over.

Sure, I know what architects 'do', what we are expected to do and what we have to do to make a living, yet I struggle to address the underlying implication of the question: how does our work make a meaningful difference in the context of the problems faced by the world at large?

I have long thought that the most rewarding way to practise architecture was simply to put one's head down and work (long hours), but lately such default insistence on perseverance feels less than gratifying. Something is up with architecture, and it is not going away. The ingrained conviction that our age-old discipline has survived many a crisis and will therefore simply outlast the latest wave of crises seems arrogant and misguided.

The solution of any problem starts with the frank acknowledgement that there is a problem. My two previous books were critiques, attempts to dismantle prevailing myths by and about the profession: *Four Walls and a Roof* targeted myths cultivated by architects, a*rchitect, verb.* took aim at myths cultivated about architects. These books were provocations, and I felt that it was ultimately up to people more creative and insightful than I am to define solutions. The one who defines the problems may not necessarily be the one best suited to propose future approaches. Writing isn't necessarily propositional; in fact, the best writing isn't.

Still the question persists: what should architects do? The more frequently it is asked, the more it becomes a statement. What *can* we do? Our field seems mired in a deep crisis of relevance. Measured against the major issues of our time – climate change, economic inequality and political instability – the 'constructive' role of architecture is at best marginal. None of the 'sustainable solutions' we devise can remotely claim to help prevent, or even limit, global warming. The housing crisis has yet to be solved by architects, and much of our work contributes to the opposite: property speculation and escalating house prices. The political relevance we attribute to our projects is routinely proven to be nil. The notion of the 'architect-statesman' is as much a form of self-aggrandizement as it is of self-delusion.

Practising architecture today comes in two flavours: foregoing principles for work or foregoing work for principles. Large architect practices serve the rich and the powerful; small practices run small jobs uncorrupted by the greed of capitalism. Less and less is there an in-between, and a seriously divided architecture profession seems to nullify any hope of a realignment.

The loss of status is predictable. No longer the creative demiurges magically conjuring up brighter futures for an audience waiting to see the light, we increasingly witness a world in which architects are being set straight. Architecture, as we know it, may be coming to an end. Construction moratoriums to help save the climate, assertions of the rights of architect-employees, a push for the shared ownership of architect practices, the public demise of former icons of the profession, belated recognition of underrepresented groups, user participation, self-building programmes, an ever larger number of non-practising architects, unease about artificial intelligence, ever tighter scrutiny of professional ethics: environmentally, financially, politically, and so on.

The architecture profession only has itself to blame. For too long it has inhabited a space of denial. Our highly self-conscious discipline is not one for self-reflection. The larger societal issues that impact architecture – the same issues that impact any other profession – were none of our business. That is, until the world made them our business. In no uncertain terms. Time has finally caught up with architecture, only to expose it as being out of touch. Are we capable of a much-needed introspection? Are we strong enough to endure the merciless outing of our futile concerns and ingrained biases? Can an old craft put itself at the service of a new relevance?

There is a treatment in clinical psychology called 'exposure therapy' which helps patients to overcome their fears by creating a controlled environment in which the possibility of avoiding these fears is temporarily taken away. The crux of the treatment is that cure and ailment are recognized as flipsides of the same coin, that the only logical course of forward action is the acknowledgement of previous inaction, that the answer to 'what to do?' is simply 'to do that which has been avoided'.

No debunking of myths this time. *Architecture Against Architecture* is a book about uncomfortable realities that, if left unaddressed, will inevitably get the better of our profession over time. A manifesto for the future of architecture.

Reinier de Graaf, 1 May 2025

Architecture Against Architecture: A Manifesto

Something is brewing in the world of architecture.

Calls to stop building, the downfall of starchitects, the formation of labour unions, appeals to change the way architecture firms are owned, users who will no longer be ignored, the advance of AI, the untenable authority of architects well beyond retirement age, iconic buildings embroiled in money laundering, prestigious firms being called out over working for dictators, public apologies from figure heads, and so on.

The architecture profession is at war with the present. Grotesque seem the iconic structures which have marked the twenty-first century, misguided the overblown regard for those who engage in them, and futile the unwavering belief that, despite all evidence to the contrary, architecture in its current form continues to represent a force for the good.

Rife is the lip service paid to good causes. Which architect has not professed a profound awareness of environmental issues? Which architect does not share a deep concern for the people? Which architect has not sought the advance of the underprivileged? Which architect has not apologized recently? The more extensive the demonstrations of virtue from architects, the sorrier the state of architecture. How did a discipline so emphatically dedicated to modernization become so stubbornly resistant to being modernized itself?

To break the deadlock, two things must be acknowledged:

I. Architecture in its current form has lost all credibility.

II. It is high time that architects openly, in the face of the whole world, commit to a fresh start. If architects wish to be relevant, architecture must be wholly reinvented.

To this end, this book offers the following, two-part manifesto:

Part I, 'Architects', addresses the long-overdue reorganization of architect practices themselves. It would serve architects well if, before preaching to others, they put their own house in order!

Part II, 'Architecture', urges the realignment of architects' preoccupations to the pressing issues of the world at large. The world depends not on architecture; architecture depends on the world.

'Science now finds there can be ample for all, but only if the sovereign fences are completely removed!'[1] In the context of rising inequality, mounting political tensions and the ever more pressing effects of climate change, Richard Buckminster Fuller's words resonate more than ever. Meanwhile the world turns, as does the world of architecture – hostage to vested interests and the seemingly irresolvable conflicts between them. What is to be done? The fourteen chapters of this book explore the logical conclusions urged by the burning issues of our time, the tough choices ahead, and the course of action that must follow.

I

Architects

1

Firms, Not Founders

Who would have thought? The man whose work Barack Obama once described as 'genius pure and simple',[1] 'one of the great architectural visionaries of our time',[2] one of the leading architects of his generation,[3] who connects Africa to the world and the world to Africa,[4] a champion of diversity in a white profession . . . the only architect ever to realize a church, synagogue and mosque as part of a single project,[5] whose built work includes the Nobel Peace Center, the National Museum of African American History and Culture as well as private residences for artist Chris Ofili, fashion designer Alexander McQueen, photographer Jürgen Teller and actor Ewan McGregor . . . Louis I. Kahn Visiting Professor at the University of Pennsylvania, Kenzo Tange Professor in Architecture at Harvard Graduate School of Design, Foreign Honorary Member of the American Academy of Arts and Letters . . . winner of the Royal Institute of British Architects (RIBA) Gold Medal, the American Institute of Architects (AIA)

Award for Excellence in Architecture, the Thomas Jefferson Memorial Award, the Louis I. Khan Memorial Award, the TIME100 Impact Award . . . knighted by the British Crown, appointed to the Order of Merit: Sir David Adjaye OBE, caught in the eye of a perfect storm.

The Pritzker Prize – the so-called 'Nobel Prize' of architecture – is the most prestigious trophy missing from Adjaye's list so far. Most likely, it will remain that way. On 4 July 2023, in an article in the *Financial Times*, three women accused the architect of sexual misconduct and spoke of a toxic work culture in his office that had gone unchecked for years.[6] Within a matter of hours the news snowballed into a global scandal. By the end of that same day, there was probably no architect, no client, no architecture student, or any person otherwise related to the profession, who hadn't taken notice. The damage was done – as it seemed, irreversibly.

The world of architecture loves to celebrate its heroes. Until they don't. David Adjaye's seemingly untouchable status gave way to public scorn in all but a single morning; his career was tainted, probably for good, and the future of his once thriving firm was suddenly precarious.

Adjaye's public defence hardly helped matters: 'I am ashamed to say that I entered into relationships which, though entirely consensual, blurred the boundaries between my professional and personal lives. I am deeply sorry. To restore trust and accountability, I will be immediately seeking professional help in order to learn from these mistakes to ensure that they never happen again.'[7] More succinctly: 'I didn't do anything wrong, but I'll seek help.' Questioned by the *New York Times*, Adjaye, voiced by a 'communications and crisis firm' hired for the occasion, declined to explain what that help might involve, describing it as 'a personal matter'.[8]

The allegations shocked the world of architecture and beyond, perhaps not so much because of what exactly did or (according to Adjaye) did not take place, but rather because of everything the architect had come to stand for and had now violated. Not only did Adjaye personify racial emancipation – according to some, he played a pivotal role in the changing perceptions of an entire continent – he had also been a strong advocate when it came to closing the 'gender gap' in architecture, expressing his embarrassment over the pay gap multiple times. In 2017, speaking to *Dezeen* at the Interior Design Show in Toronto, he said: 'I find it exhausting that women are still fighting for gender parity. I find it embarrassing to be really honest. We're in the twenty-first century. This is such an old story; we should be way past this. I'm embarrassed, as a male.'[9] When, in a conversation recorded for the 2021 RIBA Royal Gold Medal ceremony, the head of Adjaye Associates' London studio, Lucy Tilley, congratulated Adjaye on becoming Sir David, she was close to tears.[10]

But then the news broke. Each of the three women who had accused Adjaye was a black single mother, and there was little in their history to suggest that they had joined his business for any other reason than that they believed in his mission to transform architecture in Africa and showcase black talent. These were simple facts that left any conventional defence moot. Their speaking out could not be dismissed as a racially motivated slur, nor as a competitive attack motivated by envy. The women stood for everything Adjaye stood for and had spent his life fighting for.

Adjaye's problem was not so much that he was exposed as a philanderer, but as someone apparently in conflict with his own cause. Not the best condition under which to wage a counter-offensive. For Adjaye, going the Trump route was not an option: after an extensive commitment to the good, no 'bad boy' image would save him. As so often, having the perfect reputation proved double-edged, its slightest tainting equalling its outright crushing. David Adjaye was in trouble.

What ensued was predictable, even if the speed with which things unfolded made the fallout against Richard Meier – accused of similar misconduct five years earlier in the first high-profile #MeToo case in architecture – seem modest in comparison. The Studio Museum in Harlem was the first to distance itself from its architect. Not long after, the Africa Institute in Sharjah, Vermont's Shelburne Museum, Princeton University Art Museum, National Museums Liverpool, and Multnomah County Library in Oregon also cancelled their projects. Work on the British Holocaust Memorial was suspended, and Dan Gilbert's real estate firm Bedrock stated that it was evaluating its ongoing association with Adjaye. (There has been no update since July 2023.) Adjaye himself walked away from a redevelopment project in Chicago for real estate developer Fern Hill. He also stepped down from his roles as architectural advisor to London Mayor Sadiq Khan and as a trustee of London's Serpentine Gallery.

And then there were the consequences for Adjaye's office itself. Inevitably, layoffs followed. *Architects' Journal* reported that almost half of Adjaye Associates' 110-strong workforce in London lost their jobs. The office declined to confirm whether the figure was accurate.[11] Once out, former employees spoke of a culture of abuse ingrained in the office. 'There was a reverential tone [towards Adjaye]', one of them told the magazine. 'It was very messianic . . . We used to joke about one of the directors being a "high priest"', she continued. Another former employee from the New York office confessed: 'For many of us, Adjaye Associates was this kind of fantasy of diversity within architecture.' A fellow former New York employee wrote on LinkedIn: 'I believe the fish rots from the head . . . it was clear to me that the biggest problem at Adjaye Associates was David Adjaye.'[12]

The allegations might be viewed as an exception, but the stature of someone like David Adjaye in the world of architecture surely isn't. After art and literature, architecture is *the* field to grant individual men and women (more men than women) a near mythical status. Nowhere is this more evident than in the way the architecture profession pays tribute to itself. Just as in literature and art, awards in architecture are prolific. Some of the awards are given to projects or offices, but many are granted on a personal basis, to office founders or to figureheads – in architecture there is rarely a difference – for what is presumed to be their achievement and their achievement only. If we take Adjaye as an example, thirty of the ninety-four awards granted for the firm's work went to him personally, trumped only by Zaha Hadid, who was awarded 67 out of 172 – more than a third.

More than any other award, it is the Pritzker Prize (the award Adjaye didn't get) that cemented the idea of the architect as an individual creator into the mainstream, arguably – if the praise bestowed on its laureates is anything to go by – to the point of caricature.

Kevin Roche is 'no easy man to describe: an innovator who does not worship innovation for itself, a professional unconcerned with trends, a quiet, humble man who conceives and executes great works, a generous man of strictest standards for his own work'.[13] 'Son, grandson, husband and father of architects, Gottfried Böhm has reason to recognize the nourishment that traditional ways and means provide in architecture, as in all the arts.'[14] 'Every architect who aspires to greatness must in some sense reinvent architecture; conceive new solutions; develop a special design character; find a new aesthetic vocabulary. Portzamparc's work exhibits all these characteristics.'[15] 'Renzo Piano's work exemplifies that rare melding of art, architecture, and engineering in a truly remarkable synthesis. His intellectual curiosity and problem-solving techniques are as broad and far ranging as those of two earlier masters of his native land, Leonardo da Vinci and Michelangelo.'[16]

The glory of a few implies the invisibility of many. While meant to recognize the importance of architects and their achievements, architecture awards, and the Pritzker Prize in particular, in fact expose one of the most feudal tendencies of the profession. Much has been done to deviate from the default profile of laureates. Women architects have been promoted, the profile of emerging architects has been raised, and multiple architects of minority groups, racial or otherwise, have been awarded some of the most prestigious prizes in the business. While all good and justified, this has hardly taken care of the real problem: the unrelenting focus on the individual.

The feudality of architecture resides not so much in its lack of diversity as in its lack of diverse recognition. How much can credibly be attributed to a single individual? Great is the

Lord and most worthy of praise; his greatness no one can fathom. Given the gargantuan effort it takes to realize a(ny) building, the excessive laureation for some inevitably implies the consistent ignoration of others – the vast majority, in fact.

Even the music and film industries – the domains in which by far the most awards are given (and arguably the domains of the greatest worshipping after religion) – tend to think of themselves in more collective terms than architecture does. In addition to performers, the Grammys celebrate songwriters and producers as stars in their own right, while the Oscars have twenty-three categories including Actress in a Leading Role, Actor in a Supporting Role, Cinematography, Costume Design, Directing, Writing, Music, Visual Effects, Production Design, and Makeup and Hairstyling.

The Oscars are by no means a gratuitous example. Where art and literature might still be categorized as 'individual expressions' – the work of a single mind done in solitude – architecture, like film, cannot. It is the great dirty secret of architecture, particularly contemporary architecture, that individual creation doesn't really exist in the way it is often imagined. The stereotypical image of the maestro juggling the 6B pencil to produce key sketches to be handed down for execution by mere mortals in the drawing room does not even qualify as a caricature; it is a phantasy.

A figurehead is 'a head or chief (of an organization or country) with little or no authoritative power' – a leader in name only. Insofar as it applies to figureheads in architecture, the description is uncannily revealing. Towards the end of the last century, particularly in the 1990s, the business of architecture underwent profound changes on multiple fronts. Globalization created a global playing field, impacting both the number of projects done at any given time and their geographical spread. Signature practices, and especially their figureheads, acquired global fame.

The notion of the 'starchitect' came into being – a status further galvanized by the arrival of the World Wide Web. The lone genius of the twentieth century gave way to the omniscient figurehead of the twenty-first. Not surprisingly, the cultural or societal status of architects escalated in perfect tandem with the escalation of both the workload and reach of their practices.

To list a few examples: In the 1950s, at the peak of his production, Eero Saarinen's office, head of one of the most successful international offices of the postwar years, completed twenty projects. The portfolio of American architecture firm SOM grew from eight realized projects in the 1950s to over 400 today.[17] Le Corbusier designed his first building at eighteen and kept working until the day before he died. In a career spanning fifty-nine years, he completed seventy-nine buildings. By comparison, Foster + Partners has completed 426 projects within a much shorter period.

An X-ray of the global reach of practices shows a similar picture: In the 1950s, six out of SOM's eight projects were in the US. Today, the firm operates in eight countries on three continents.[18] Foster realized his first building outside the UK in 1985. Currently, as of their website, the firm has 397 completed projects in forty-six countries on six continents, including ninety-seven projects in the UK. OMA didn't have any projects realized until the mid-eighties. Today, the partnership has 262 projects in twenty-six countries on five continents, with thirty-five of those projects in the Netherlands.

In addition to larger and more dispersed project portfolios, the new epoch also brought increased pressure on the projects themselves. With the global embrace of the market economy after the fall of the Berlin Wall and the subsequent collapse of the Soviet Union, architecture firms entered a new phase of global competition. No longer was work granted nationally, through tried relations or repeat commissions; it was now awarded through (invited) competitions or international public tenders. The criteria associated with these – in terms of financial guarantees, liability, insurance, and so on – meant that architecture firms inevitably had to increase in size. And as they grew, so did the entrepreneurial risk. With little or no compensation offered for work during the tender stage, a substantial part of a project often had to be done simply in order to acquire it. Since the 1990s, the stakes of the 'business' of architecture have been raised considerably.

The rat race that affected the economy of offices equally applied to the design of projects. The need to compete globally has trapped architecture in a global race for attention. The 1990s marked the beginning of so-called iconic architecture (as well as the rebranding of all former architectures as such), which propelled the increasing hybridization of architecture and marketing. If the central pursuit of marketing is to generate the largest possible degree of product variation from the greatest possible repetition of a standard formula, then three decades' worth of architectural 'icons' embody that pursuit perfectly. Where the building boom of twentieth-century postwar Europe could partly meet demand by relying on the repetition of certain building typologies, the global building boom of the twenty-first century must reinvent the wheel with every new building, every competition, every tender.

Another major change affecting the architecture profession has been the advance of digital technology. Ever since the late 1980s, computer-aided design (CAD) tools (AutoCAD, 1982; MicroStation, 1985; MiniCAD, 1985, later renamed Vectorworks) have steadily eradicated forests of drawing boards and helped reduce factory-size drawing rooms to the size of an average office floor as we know it today. The invention of the World Wide Web and HTML combined with the emergence of internet service providers (ISPs) at the beginning of the 1990s expanded the horizon of references to virtually every corner of the world and every period in history in an instant.

More important perhaps than the effect on the execution of projects is the effect of digital technology on their inception. More than mere tools, software and access to information have become integral parts of the design process – an evolution which has only been taken to a greater extreme with the advent of 3D modelling (3D Studio, 1990, later renamed 3D Studio Max and now Autodesk 3ds Max; Maya, 1998; Rhino, 1998; SketchUp, 2000), building information modelling (ArchiCAD, 1987; Autodesk Revit, 2000), parametric design (Grasshopper, 2007), virtual reality (Oculus Rift, 2013; HTC Vive, 2016, augmented reality (Apple Vision Pro, 2023) and artificial intelligence (DALL-E, 2021; Midjourney, 2022). When it comes to architecture design, 'thinking outside of the box' has acquired all too literal a meaning. AI may well represent the next step.

The above three revolutions – the increased number of simultaneously handled projects, their geographical spread, and the emergence of digital tools of production – have changed the process of architecture beyond recognition. In so doing, they have also profoundly changed the way architecture offices are run. No longer can they be governed (let alone controlled) by a single individual. Even in a medium-sized office, the number of concurrent operations will exceed the thought capacity of a single mastermind. Travel tends to be demanding and ultimately even the stamina of the best-preserved body has its limits. No amount of golf, tennis, running or swimming does anything to change that.

When it comes to the last revolution – the digital revolution – most founders, figureheads and even senior staff of architecture offices are of a generation that, at best, can hope to be tolerated spectators in a space where essentially all the productive work is done by others. More than anything, the digital revolution has finalized the divorce between the production of an office and those leading it. With the likely exception of Patrik Schumacher, the current principal of Zaha Hadid Architects, no architect running an office today can understand even the basics of these technologies. Those who own the tools of production are the ones least familiar with their inner workings. Alienation ensues, this time not between the alienated masses and the machines they operate, but between the machines and those in charge.

The last drawing board left the office on my first working day at OMA (2 January 1996). From then on, all projects were to be drawn up on computers. It soon became clear that models could be made digitally just as easily – and perhaps more effectively – as they had been with cardboard, foam or resin. Had I entered the office a day earlier I might have been useful. But in no way did this impede my career. I was gradually promoted up the ranks and eventually got to co-own the practice. Career progression can be a funny thing: the more I climbed, the more I also felt removed from the 'real work', confined to evaluating, critiquing and selecting from the huge production harvest routinely emerging from the office's printers, watching things taking shape on screens, witnessing plots evolve, pretty much the way they do on TV. Authority at the expense of remoteness. There are architects much older than me who continue to practise today (more about that in Chapter 4). What applies to me must apply to them in the extreme. Theirs is an alienation I can only imagine.

Notwithstanding such tragi-comic confessions, the general focus on figureheads seems unrelenting. The dominant presence of founders tends to continue well after they have transferred majority ownership of their firms to others, and sometimes even after ownership has been surrendered entirely. The economic success of architecture firms begins and ends with reputations, particularly with that of a founder, commonly assumed to be the sole proprietor of that reputation. That notion prevails externally as well as internally, inside architecture offices themselves.

The presumption that founders are the sole point of reference is a major liability when it comes to the future evolution of architecture firms (or even just their catching up with the present). The drawbacks of absolute rule may be commonly accepted in (civilized) politics, but in architecture it is all too often the default mode. Fame doesn't help. The greater the celebrity, the greater the veneration; the greater the veneration, the greater the pre-emptive servility.

Ironically, the keenest proponents of this system are often the employees of architecture firms themselves, worried perhaps that their house of cards might collapse if it is disturbed – that a revolution within the profession might touch them too, and not necessarily for the better. All too frequently we hear that without its figurehead an office would be nothing, that there would be no office, that the figurehead *is* the office. Still, there are many more architects than there are figureheads, and, as David Adjaye's ongoing troubles show, even the life of a figurehead isn't necessarily a bed of roses. When push comes to shove, the system can be as cruel to its (supposed) beneficiaries as to those condemned to live in the shadows.

Status grants to power the aura of being unconditional; if power corrupts, then unconditional power corrupts unconditionally. It is by no means a coincidence that most allegations of toxic work cultures occur in fields that worship their heroes, fields that make a habit of branding collective achievements as individual successes. The more the boundaries between collective and individual achievements are blurred, the greater the impunity with which that habit can continue.

While this is particularly true of firms named after their founder, it is by no means limited to them. Architecture is a business incorrigibly equated with individuals: no matter how far firms expand, grow, diversify, portray themselves as collectives or obscure the identity of individuals behind three-letter acronyms, nothing serves to undo the persistent notion that ultimately a body of work can only be the brainchild of one man or woman. There is probably no other profession in which perception and reality are as far apart as in architecture.

More than an argument from fairness, however, there is a business argument to be made. Succession within architect practices is a notoriously difficult and painful process. Even succession by namesake offspring is by no means a guarantee for continuity of business. The larger the reputation of the founder, the more difficult the continuation of what they have founded. The essence of all business lies in the transient nature of its leadership. The more the architecture business is equated with figureheads, the more figureheads will be bad for the business of architecture in the long run.

The focus on figureheads is holding architecture hostage, clouding both a meaningful interpretation of its past and a productive speculation on its future. Not unlike the economy of nineteenth-century England, architecture is stuck in a curious situation in which modern practices continue to unfold in the context of feudal traditions. The more we continue these servile traditions, the more we, as a profession, will run into a dead end. The greater the veneration of architects, the more rapid the demise of their trade. People pass away; a profession does not.

The spectre can only be warded off for so long. It is high time we openly recognized, and embraced with pride, the true nature of our work. Architects are dead; long live architecture! Promote firms, not their founders; recognize projects, not their authors; reward initiatives, not their sponsors. End the focus on figureheads!

Adjaye Associates is slowly finding its way back into the business. Earlier this year, it announced a new structure for the firm. As Richard Meier did before him, Adjaye distanced himself from the company. Lucy Tilley, Pascale Sablan and Kofi Bio have been appointed CEOs of the London, New York and Accra offices, respectively, while Adjaye himself remains as creative director.

No legal charges were pressed, and it doesn't seem they will be. However sad for all involved, perhaps it is important not to view Adjaye's case as just an instance of presumed personal excess. Somehow, the nature of the alleged behaviour is the least interesting aspect of the whole episode. Perhaps Adjaye's ultimate crime was the destruction of his own myth. In the eyes of the world, his big flaw might well be that he proved human after all, prone, like all of us, to the abuse of power when too much power is given.

A fourth act in the tragedy – the miraculous recovery and triumph of the protagonist against the odds – remains pending. It is unlikely that will change, and, even if it did, it would scarcely undo the damage done in the process. Richard Meier allegedly spends his days at home painting, and Sir David Adjaye OBE will never be what he was.

2

Architects, Unite!

My uncle was a Union Man, at the forefront of strikes in the Port of Rotterdam during the 1970s. More often on the barricades than at work, he fought for higher pay, proper compensation of overtime, better workplace conditions, or whatever else merited uproar in his eyes and those of his colleagues. They turned up in large numbers, in solidarity, united in their determination to resist the exploitation of themselves and everyone like them. 'WORKER POWER' read the banner stuck to the front of his two-horsepower car.

A picture of the scene made the front page of a local newspaper, much to the dismay of my mother, aunt, grandmother and grandfather, who worried about his career prospects more than they rejoiced over any short-term victories. Not me! With his thick curly hair and long beard, he had the appeal of a messiah. Jesus Christ Superstar! All of twenty-one years of age, my uncle was a hero, a rebel *with* a cause, and not shy to voice it – incessantly, ferociously, fearlessly. He even rattled his own union, fearful as they were of how his fiery rhetoric might affect ongoing negotiations with employers. But as far as he was concerned, the union didn't go anywhere near far enough.

'Economic crisis' invariably served as a reason not to give in to workers' demands, but the figures indicated otherwise. Profits in the Port of Rotterdam were at an all-time high, and had been for some time. What fools did they take them for? Money was being made, and dock workers deserved their rightful share! Their work was not to be taken for granted. Men like my uncle – nothing moved without them. Labour was a force, and the organized withholding of it served as a reminder to anyone who might forget.

'"Architectural Workers United" helps overworked and underpaid designers speak up for themselves.'[1] In September 2022, the first ever union in a privately owned architect practice became a fact – in Brooklyn, New York, at Bernheimer Architects, a practice of twenty or so people working on affordable housing and small retail projects. Better late than never. With the profession's long hours, low wages and limited job security, concern over the working conditions at architecture firms seemed long overdue.

Architectural Workers United's (AWU) website lists five reasons to support the organization: 1) 'because three weekends in a row doesn't equal one compensation day'; 2) 'because this industry will never pay my student loans'; 3) 'because the environment deserves better care than my exhaustion'; 4) 'because iterations aren't free'; and 5) 'because even though buildings are machines, I am not!'[2]

The prime catalyst for the group's coming into being was the murder of George Floyd. To AWU, as to many in America,

Floyd's death, more than simply providing evidence of racism within the police force, served as a reason to examine the injustices embedded in all existing power structures. By implication, that included the power structures underpinning the architecture profession too. The injustices were many and they were evident: from the racial and gender imbalance within architecture firms, to their elitist hiring practices, to the substandard working conditions of those who eventually do manage to get hired – long hours, uncompensated overtime, late nights, lack of a proper work-life balance, and low wages relative to the level of education.

Various media outlets have summarized AWU's mission as an effort to set right an industry tainted by long hours and low pay. Stripped of undue claims of suffering, the two main demands of the architectural workforce are perfectly straightforward, mundane even, and not dissimilar to those in other sectors of employment. Indeed, with their recently formed union being a subsidiary of the International Association of Machinists and Aerospace Workers (IAMAW), architect-employees at Bernheimer find themselves in the good company of other 'workers'.

Founded in 1888, and with a current membership of nearly 600,000 across 200 industries, the IAMAW is one of the oldest and largest labour unions in North America. It represents workers at companies as diverse as Harley-Davidson, Southwest Airlines, Boeing, Pratt & Whitney, Freightliner, Tennessee Valley Authority and the Bureau of Engraving and Printing. Its mission statement is as comprehensive as the range of sectors it represents: At IAMAW, 'we believe that given the state of work in our current world, people must unite to obtain the full reward of their labour . . . that working people should exercise their rights cooperatively and economically for the benefit of all people.'[3] Consequently, the organization pledges to 'work for our Members to continue to preserve and grow the IAM on the basis of solidarity and justice, and to strive for a higher standard of living for all people who work'.[4]

Like any union, IAMAW is in a permanent drive for expansion, forever eager to incorporate the next field of employment in need of better pensions, medical insurance, paid vacations, sick pay or shift differentials. In 1991, the union incorporated the Pattern Makers' League of North America into its ranks. Later, in 2005, it merged with the Transportation Communications International Union (TCU). On 7 September 2008, members of the union initiated a strike against Boeing, citing concerns over outsourcing, job security, wages and benefits.[5] In December 2013, the IAMAW attempted to organize workers at an Amazon fulfilment centre located in Middletown, Delaware.[6]

The union's most recent expansion into architecture, landscape architecture and urban design firms is perhaps not surprising. The field has been steadily highlighting its own flaws over the last few years, almost as a cry for help. Just as the unions have found their way to the world of architecture, the world of architecture seems to have found its way to the unions. Affiliated with IAMAW, the AWU grew out of a nonprofit group called the Architecture Lobby, founded by Yale architecture professor Peggy Deamer in 2013. Although not a union itself, the Lobby advocates for the value of work within the architecture industry, calling for major changes to the way the industry operates, including an end to unpaid labour, payment of a living wage and compensation for pervasive overtime, and remuneration from clients that matches the value of the work architecture firms do.

Noteworthy is the connection the group makes between the quality and fairness of the built environment itself and the nature of the working practices that shape it. 'We focus on organizing for ecological justice as it relates to architectural labor, the built environment, and sustainable futures for all.'[7] Nurturing miscellaneous causes such as climate change, the transition away from fossil fuels, the fight against capitalism and the unionization of architecture firms, the Architecture Lobby presents itself as 'a grassroots organization of architectural workers that advocates for just labor practices and an equitable (built) environment'.[8]

To facilitate the organization of workers, it has set up a Unionization Working Group (UWG). The purpose of the Group is to act as a portal helping workers find their way to unions in the best and most discreet way. Its promotional slogan has distinctly Marxist overtones: 'We consider unionization to be the strongest way to push back against the increasing immiseration of work in our professions.'[9] The Architecture Lobby's website invites workers to request more information by email. All inquiries are guaranteed to be kept anonymous. Revolution starts with a whisper. The world of architecture is no exception.

The formation of the union at Bernheimer Architects was by no means a foregone conclusion. It only acquired decisive momentum in the summer of 2020, during the COVID-19 pandemic, when, removed from daily in-person contact with management, architects had the space to reflect on the broader issues surrounding their work. The initial push to unionize took shape in the form of Zoom calls and text message chains.

Unions are customary in most sectors of employment, and there is nothing unreasonable about the expectation of having a seat at the table when decisions are made that affect one's livelihood. The principle is common practice in almost any industry. But in the architecture profession this represented a seismic change. The successful unionization at Bernheimer was preceded by two failed attempts at larger firms in the same city: one at SHoP Architects in Manhattan, and an earlier one at the New York base of the Norwegian firm Snøhetta. At the latter, the proposal to unionize was put to a vote by the firm's sixty-four employees and rejected by a narrow margin (35 to 29).[10] At SHoP, the initiative was abandoned before it could come to fruition, allegedly because of serious disincentivizing from senior management.[11]

As with most unionization processes, the effort at SHoP started underground, remotely for the most part due to the pandemic, with two employees initially gauging the interest of their colleagues. For most of 2020 and 2021, their effort progressed under the radar, with guidance from the IAMAW and the support of several other architect-employees operating meanwhile under the name 'Architectural Workers United'.

In the autumn of 2021, the same two employees presented a letter to SHoP's management board laying out their plans for a union vote. At that point, they were confident of having 60 per cent of the staff on board. What ensued was an aggressive anti-union campaign from SHoP's management, who argued that unionization would affect the firm's ability to secure new clients and thus be bad for business. A round of layoffs followed in the winter of 2022, and the two employees are no longer part of the firm. One of them got a job with IAMAW as a union organizer. The other went to work at

Bernheimer, where a union was established in September of that same year.

Given the fate of the effort at SHoP, the process at Bernheimer seems to have been surprisingly consensual. After a solemn pledge from the staff – 'We're Not Trying to Shut Down the Firm With Any of Our Demands' – the firm's principal, Andy Bernheimer, recognized the union without it having to be put to a formal vote through the National Labor Relations Board. Asked for his reasons, he replied: 'My understanding is that, as a service profession, we are hired for our talent, we are hired for our expertise, we are probably also hired relative to our cost. I have confidence that any unionization effort wouldn't affect any of those factors to the point that we would stop getting work.'[12]

Despite the consensual rhetoric, it is safe to assume that, at Bernheimer too, both staff and management took some convincing. All in all, the unionization process took three months. Most likely a substantial part of that was spent overcoming scepticism; not just from the firm's leadership – in this case only the firm's principal – but also from its employees. For many working in architecture, the idea of unionization brings a sense of discomfort, worried as people tend to be about the opinion of their superiors. Changing the status quo inevitably creates uncertainties. However, after seeing enough union cards reflecting his employees' determination to form a union, Bernheimer eventually opted for voluntary recognition rather than a formal election, making the first ever union in a privately owned architecture business a reality.

In an industry unaccustomed to labour unrest, the idea of unions is causing serious discomfort. The statement Snøhetta issued after its narrow escape is telling: 'We look forward to working together as one studio to continue building on our legacy of creativity and collaboration.'[13] Equally unfortunate was the response of the New York branch of my own firm, OMA, to the outrage provoked by a job advertisement requiring 'No 9–5 mentality'; this, it claimed, was intended to appeal to applicants with 'creativity and passion'. Such statements expose all too clearly the mindset of an industry that likes to think of itself as a happy, consensual family.

The stereotype of the exploited worker serving his bourgeois capitalist boss hardly seems to apply to the architecture profession. Overtime is endemic, but it generally happens in the absence of any explicit demand for it. Such is the pride in our work that we gladly forego self-interest (and sometimes our private lives and health) for the cause. If we are being exploited, we are so by our own free will. We exploit ourselves.

All-nighters, last-minute changes, incessant perfectionism . . . Never is the work good enough. One wonders what compels architects to work the way they do? Who are we trying to impress? Our efforts bear no relation to our clients' demands. Neither do they bear any real relation to public recognition of our work, or to the extent to which the world rewards us financially. Architecture is work. That seems obvious. But somehow that never seems to be quite enough. There is a twist to the concept of working in architecture, which doesn't seem to exist in other industries in the same way. More than work, being an architect seems to imply the notion of a selfless crusade for a higher cause, from which one ought not to be distracted by menial concerns over labour conditions or other peripheral issues. If you want to be a good architect, sacrifice is a given. That seems true of architecture, and perhaps of the creative professions in general.

Why is that?

As a profession, architecture as we know it emerged during the Italian Renaissance, when it transitioned from being the domain of master masons and builders to being the province of 'intellectuals'. Figures like Alberti, Brunelleschi and Palladio positioned themselves not just as artisans but as *architecti* – thinkers who combined mathematics, philosophy and artistic sensibility with the practical knowledge of construction. This transformation was fuelled by the patronage of powerful elites who sought to elevate architecture beyond the notion of mere craftsmanship that had prevailed in the medieval guilds. Though they were still heavily reliant on draughtsmen and builders, the shift from artisan to intellectual allowed *architecti* to claim a new professional identity, distinct from the construction trades.

This development took a particular twist in seventeenth- and eighteenth-century Britain, where it fused with a distinctly local tradition: that of the gentleman amateur. Figures like Christopher Wren, John Vanbrugh and, later, John Soane embodied this model. They were often from an elite or scholarly background rather than from a trade apprenticeship one. Architecture was seen as an extension of aristocratic pursuits, not as a means of livelihood per se. The leading architects came from miscellaneous backgrounds in mathematics, philosophy or military engineering.

Wren, for instance, did not pursue architecture until the age of thirty-three, when he was already an accomplished man of science with achievements in the fields of astronomy, optics, cosmology, mechanics, microscopy, surveying, medicine and meteorology. William Kent, architect of the revived Palladian style in England, started out as a painter and only became an architect in his forties. Richard Boyle, the 3rd Earl of Burlington and another proponent of the Palladian style, more or less accidentally developed a taste for architecture during his trips to Paris. Perhaps the most famous gentleman-turned-architect is Thomas Jefferson, third president of the United States. 'Architecture is my delight,' he once commented, 'and putting up, and pulling down, one of my favourite amusements.'[14]

What connects the Renaissance *métier* and the gentleman aesthete tradition is the separation of the architect from labour. The Renaissance architect was an intellectual distinct from masons and builders; the British gentleman-architect was an aesthete, designing buildings as an extension of his cultured upbringing. If they had employees, they remained anonymous. As the 'king's surveyor', Wren became the public face of many projects, even if we know today that the principal creative responsibility for these projects, such as 'his' fifty-two rebuilt churches, resided with others.

Britain was one of the first countries to properly formalize the architecture profession. The gentleman aesthete tradition is crucial to understanding how this took shape – particularly in terms of the profession's resistance to identifying as labour. The gentlemanly aura persisted even after the profession was formalized. The early RIBA model, for example, positioned architects as intellectuals rather than tradesmen, which helped insulate them from the more industrial models of labour organization seen in engineering or construction.

All of that changed with the formation of big practices during the successive building booms of the late nineteenth century, first in the UK and later in North America. Large armies of architect-employees came to work for a small number of architect-owners, a trend that was further escalated in the early twentieth century. Marx's analysis of labour as applied to other sectors of the economy came equally to apply to architecture: subject to the division of labour and reliant on a productive class denied ownership of the means of production. Given these realities, it becomes in every way appropriate to refer to architects as 'working class'.

It would, however, take another fifty years for architects to develop 'class consciousness', and it took nothing less than a global economic crisis for this to manifest. The first attempt to unionize architects came in 1933, with the merger of the Union of Technical Men and the United Committee of Architects, Engineers and Chemists to form the Federation of Architects, Engineers, Chemists and Technicians (FAECT). During the Great Depression, unemployment among architects and draughtsmen in the United States soared to 90 per cent. Outrage over the minimal wages for architectural and engineering draughtsmen, as published by the American Institute of Architects under the National Industrial Recovery Act (NIRA), greatly propelled the cause.

By the time FAECT was founded on 23 August 1933, tensions had been simmering in architectural and engineering offices for over a decade. Already during the 1920s, before the Wall Street Crash, draughtsmen working in large offices had been complaining about unstable employment, low wages and long hours. Their attempts to form a union, however, were steadily opposed by their architect colleagues, who found the idea of a union antithetical to the profession.[15]

The debate was further complicated by the emergence of 'the employee architect' (a class of architects employed as wage labourers by other architects) as a byproduct of the formation of big architecture firms during the previous decades. Initially, these architect-employees were inclined to side with their employers, clinging to the societal image of their occupation despite their economic misery. The tipping point came with the US government's Works Progress Administration (WPA) programme, which turned large numbers of architects into federal employees. As a result of this change, union membership was no longer taboo. In fact, federally employed architects came to form a core constituency of FAECT for much of the Great Depression.[16]

The WPA did another thing: it redefined the nature of architectural work itself. In the context of government programmes, an architect was identified as a 'technical worker', a colloquialism that had gained traction in the early twentieth century. For a union such as FAECT, the equation of architectural design with other kinds of technical work was helpful in generating solidarity between architects, engineers, chemists and technicians, and it proved to be a powerful tool in breaking any prior loyalty workers might have had to their management.

Identifying architects as technical workers also helped solidify their pact with other union workers and with working-class politics more broadly. It was for this reason that FAECT supported the United Automotive Workers (UAW) during their strikes in 1938. In working with the UAW on their campaign, FAECT argued that technical and production workers should collaborate as equals, to overcome their mutual vulnerability to exploitation by management.[17]

In retrospect, FAECT's ability to leverage the term 'technical worker' in service of cross-industry solidarity may have been crucial in exposing political bias concerning the role of technical work in relation to society at large. It also exposed the political blindness of architects in relation to their own situation. No longer could they afford to think that the burning issues of their time did not affect them. The notion of architecture as an apolitical field was effectively put on hold – at least for a while.

After the Second World War, things at FAECT started to take a turn for the worse. Like other unions, it had been spearheaded by members of the Communist Party. While their party affiliation had buoyed their efforts in the 1930s, it gutted their power in the 1940s as union leaders were red-baited by the Taft–Hartley Act, forced to testify in front of the House Un-American Activities Committee, and blacklisted from practice. Famously, Julius Rosenberg and Robert Oppenheimer were accused of Communist Party affiliation because of their FAECT membership. In 1946, FAECT was dismantled and merged into the United Office and Professional Workers of America union.[18]

Historically, efforts to promote solidarity between architects and other workers have been few and far between. Likewise with efforts to popularize the notion of architects as 'workers'. In June 1948, at its inaugural meeting in Lausanne, the International Union of Architects (UIA) discussed the organization's founding statutes. One point of contention was whether the UIA should be referred to as an association of 'progressive, democratic organizations of workers in architecture'. The Soviets and the communist Eastern Europeans argued that it should, and the decision was put to a vote. The Americans and the British abstained, while the French, Swiss, Italians and Belgians voted against, arguing that the UIA should maintain an apolitical stance and defend the status of architecture as an autonomous discipline.[19]

Politics were gradually exorcised from the architecture profession during the postwar years, and one could argue that this remains the situation today. The main voluntary associations within the profession are membership bodies that look after the interests of the architects in general, whether bosses or employees. Much like the old guilds, such bodies were designed to prevent the exploitation not of workers by their employers, but of a professional group by society at large. Organizations like the RIBA, the AIA or the BNA (Bond van Nederlandse Architecten) promote a boundless solidarity between members of the profession without ever acknowledging the vastly different situations they might be in. The recent graduate working for a minimum wage is expected to stand shoulder to shoulder with the architect-owner of a practice collecting millions in dividends.

The track record of these organizations in terms of lobbying for better earnings for architects is mixed at best. In the UK, ever since the 1970s, restrictions on monopolies and mergers have eroded the legality of mandatory fee scales. In 1982, the 'mandatory' RIBA fee scales became 'recommended' fee scales. Similarly, in 1990 in the US, the AIA was sued by the Justice Department for violating antitrust laws. More recently, the European Court of Justice (ECJ) ruled that the German HOAI (honorarium regulations for architects and engineers) had to dispense with fixed rates for architects and engineers. (The ruling has been in force since 1 January 2021.)

To the outside world, the reasoning behind architects' fee scales remains highly obscure. Fees are either based on a percentage of construction costs, with only a peripheral relation to the complexity of the work at hand, or on manpower schedules with hourly rates that bear little or no relation to the wages actually paid. It seems that, without hard proof of the actual 'cost out' for architecture firms in the form of fair (and paid) wages, any fight for higher fees is a lost cause from the outset.

Another factor that complicates things is the changing nature of architect employment itself. With the rise of the freelancer there are ever fewer proper employment contracts. In the US, 42 per cent of all architects are freelancers.[20] Italy, the birthplace of the architect, has the largest number of architects in Europe (30 per cent of the total). Five years after graduation, fewer than 25 per cent of architecture students have a permanent contract. The rest are either freelancers or employed on so-called 'atypical contracts'.[21] Thanks to Legislative Decree 81/2015, members of Italy's Chamber of Architects are exempt from a law that prohibits businesses from sending more than 90 per cent of their invoices to the same client.[22] Thirty-four per cent of architects in Italy earn less than €9,000 annually.[23]

In Belgium, the European country where the freelance phenomenon is at its most acute, only 2 per cent of architects work as employees.[24] In order to obtain a licence from the Belgian Chamber of Architects, aspiring architects have to undertake a two-year internship, which they can do as a freelancer, an employee or as a public servant.[25] Comparing the cost for a licensed architect to mentor an intern on the payroll (€20,000 per annum) to that of employing a freelancer

(€16,000 per annum), it becomes obvious why the freelance status in Belgium is so prevalent.[26]

Sure, a freelancer can claim to be an independently operating architect – the holy grail for many. But notwithstanding the societal standing that comes with that, being a freelancer is mostly a way of trading down. Job security is lower than ever, and the atomized relation between architects and the firms they work for renders any hope of a workforce acting in solidarity an illusion. It is every (wo)man acting for themselves.

As a freelancer, the architect is neither a worker nor the proponent of a liberal profession. Architects become a disenfranchised class of their own, unable to exercise their labour as a collective force. If nobody is an employee, a union no longer has an employment regime to oppose. The ongoing unionization may well be a race against the clock – a pre-emptive strike against the rise of firms without employees. A neck-and-neck race between the pride of being self-employed and the erosion of any given rights.

The honest view of architects as workers remains a precarious one. Architects tend not to identify with other workers and even less do they admit to feeling exploited. That hardly means there *is* no exploitation. On the contrary: it indicates how deeply exploitation is ingrained in our profession. Denied any form of professional solidarity, architecture firms engage in a race to the bottom, jumping at clients' requests, hoping to gain an advantage over their competitors, who, in turn, jump even faster. Make no mistake: the unfavourable working conditions at architecture firms are a direct reflection of the fragility of our discipline in general.

More than a threat, the recent push towards unionization is a wake-up call – a first step in ensuring the protection of the discipline as a whole, an annoying but much-needed obstacle in the context of this race to the bottom. Think of the benefits to the architecture profession if it were properly recognized as labour; imagine the power it could wield if it organized itself accordingly. A stronger profession begins with a strengthening of the position of the workforce. Welcome labour unions; they are but a small step!

Strikes intensified at the Port of Rotterdam throughout the 1970s, resulting in an increasingly bitter standoff between bosses and workers, and the repeated deployment of police in large numbers. My uncle eventually gave up his job as a dock worker to become an electrician. His fight was continued by others. The outcome remains inconclusive. In the decades following, the port became increasingly less reliant on human labour. People were replaced by robots – cheaper and not as vocal. A once militant workforce became silent. In the end, technology did what no police squad could accomplish; an early warning of what might be in store for architects.

3

Co-everything

We met in the winter of 2018, at a symposium at Yale titled 'Rebuilding Architecture'. Its theme: a redefinition of architecture 'beyond form, fame, and social *ir*responsibility'. As the poster put it: the aim was to shift 'the basic tenets that keep architecture from being socially relevant, politically powerful, financially rewarding, and personally fulfilling'.[1] The world of architecture was broken and in need of fixing. The event was scheduled to last two days.

He spoke on day two, dedicated to exploring new models that 'move beyond client-driven work' and that make work more than 'neo-liberal fulfilment'.[2] Political activism at Ivy League universities tends to be articulated in the strangest of terminologies. Although few of those attending looked like they had ever experienced the joys of 'neo-liberal fulfilment', the audience seemed unanimous in its rejection. As did the speaker. His talk carried the title 'Morality, Decency and Good Manners', the irony of which proved to be nil. Like all other participants, his commitment to the good was total and his belief in the premise of the symposium absolute.

I remember being surprised. Among the crowd of academics, the speaker's resumé felt strangely out of place. Not that it was of no relevance to the subject at hand – the practice of architecture – but rather because that practice commonly tends to be debated by those who have never engaged in it. But this man had. He was a man from the field – the only person in the room who might have a vague idea of what he was talking about.

His name was Chris Stewart ('call me Chris!') and he headed – although, given the nature of what he was 'heading', that might already qualify as a misnomer – an architect practice called Collective Architecture. Collective Architecture is a worker cooperative, which at the time had been equally owned by its employees for more than ten years. He explained how the practice functioned, how each architect had complete responsibility for the design and management of their projects, client liaisons and fee decisions. There were no ranks and no hierarchies; all involved had equal rights and responsibilities. If anyone decided to leave, the company automatically bought back their shares at their intrinsic value. Tradition had it that farewell cakes were modelled on the outgoing member's most recent project. (A substantial part of Chris's presentation consisted of pastry mimicking the form of buildings.)

I remember being taken with the self-evident nature of the endeavour. It seemed only natural for all architect practices to follow suit. The set-up of the practice resembled that of a small law firm in which each lawyer takes care of their own share of cases, generates part of the turnover and shares in the profits. Like such law firms, the Collective Architecture set-up could be described as a leaderless but nonetheless highly organized union of educated professionals. Chris showed us their pictures: decent people without exception.

I was impressed. That is, I was until I started paying attention to the accompanying imagery: a never-ending jumble of utterly nondescript projects, varying from inconspicuous housing projects to thirteen-in-a-dozen community centres, the occasional library and a 'Park Hub'. The well-intended nature of these projects made it difficult to be critical, but it was equally difficult to discern how the look and feel of them would have been different had no architect been involved. Each project seemed to have gone through so much community consultation that any edge, any spice, had been carefully 'consulted away'. Perhaps that was the whole point: the projects of Collective Architecture were collective in the sense that they also catered to the sum of all common taste.

I thought of our own firm, which, after almost two decades of slavishly towing the line, I could now rightfully call mine too (something Chris emphatically did not want to do when talking about his). We did good work, so I thought, but I also knew intimately the circumstances from which that work emerged: absolute hell! Chris's world by contrast seemed like an implausible version of heaven. The whole experience left me decidedly confused. I felt over- and underwhelmed at the same time. Inexorably fair conditions went hand in hand with what I can only describe as a staggeringly mediocre output. It was proof of the possibility of work, rather than the work itself, that seemed to be at the heart of this story. The price to be paid for social justice within the trade was the disappearance of the trade altogether. Not exactly an uplifting prospect. I needed to know more.

❧

Why are so few architecture firms actually owned by the architects who work for them? Architecture is a collective endeavour, yet that is hardly ever reflected in the ownership of architect practices. Firms continue to be (majority) owned by their founders or (co-)owned by the founders and a small group of seasoned collaborators around them. Strangely so, perhaps. What greater incentive to working is there than working for oneself? Especially when it concerns creative work. Equity aside, it is not unreasonable to presume that the collective ownership of architect practices would spark an unprecedented architectural creativity.

That realization is beginning to dawn, so it seems. Employee-owned architect practices have become a bit of a thing lately. Somewhat counterintuitively perhaps, a lot of them have emerged in Anglo-Saxon countries, not a part of the world typically thought of as having a great affinity for 'worker collectives'. Yet in fact it is those countries that have promoted employee ownership of businesses on a wider scale, not just in architecture.

More than a countercultural move against the system, this trend seems to be a product of the system itself. Not altogether surprisingly. Capitalism is based on private enterprise, that is, the competition between privately owned businesses. At the same time, it demands the continuity of business in general. It is inevitable that these two principles will come into friction at some point. The private ownership of businesses – by individuals – by definition represents a problem vis-à-vis the pressures on their continued performance. Individuals are mortal; businesses ought not to be.

The limitations of family-owned businesses, in which ownership is passed on by inheritance, to be continued ad infinitum, have been well documented since as long ago as the Industrial Revolution. It was only a matter of time before businesses themselves, like property, goods and services before them, had to be separated from individuals – passed on from owner to owner, more often multiple owners at the same time, treated as tradable assets, subject to mergers and acquisitions, publicly owned when large enough, listed on the stock exchange, with their performance watched over by owners and prospective owners alike. In modern economies, private enterprise is a public affair.

In the UK there has been the emergence of Employee-Owned Trusts (EOTs). Although this type of ownership structure stops short of a full distribution of company shares among employees, it does arguably represent a model for the genuine collectivization of businesses. Shares are held in a trust for the benefit of employees, who can join the trust without providing advance financing by themselves. Currently, this type of ownership is the main form of employee ownership in the UK, which may serve as some evidence of its success. Its widespread adoption indicates just how pressing the discussion about more enduring forms of business ownership has become.

Although the UK has a longer history of various forms of employee ownership, propagated by both Labour and Conservative governments, the idea of EOTs acquired definitive momentum with the advent of the Conservative/Liberal Democrat coalition government in 2010. In the autumn of 2012 it released the so-called Nuttall Review, which aimed to identify 'the barriers to employee ownership and help find the solutions to knock them down'.[3] Written by the government's independent advisor Graeme Nuttall, the Review advocated employee ownership in the form of trusts, as they were considered to provide a financially realistic structure to facilitate employee buyouts. To encourage employee ownership through EOTs, the Review further advocated several tax incentives, which indeed became part of UK tax law in 2014.

At the core of the policy was the idea that employee ownership incentivizes employee engagement and thus raises productivity. This is also evident from the report's full title: 'Sharing Success: The Nuttall Review of Employee Ownership'. The then employment minister Norman Lamb is quoted on the subject: 'A worker who has a financial and personal stake in a company will take more responsibility for its success. The evidence shows that this is reflected in the economic strength of such companies: lower absenteeism, a happier workforce and therefore less staff turnover, higher profitability. These companies also tend to be more resilient in tough economic times.'[4] In Graeme Nuttall's own words: 'The longevity of companies with employee ownership is impressive. Employee ownership is an adaptable concept and whatever the business or the stage a business has reached, employee ownership can work well.'[5]

Perhaps the most important indicator of its success is how the idea of the EOT has acquired traction outside the UK. Companies in the US, Canada and Australia have also adopted it as a business model, and there is apparently interest in Denmark too.

In the US, the equivalent of the EOT is the Employee Stock Ownership Plan (ESOP), which became prevalent in the US around the same time, and for similar reasons: to give a boost to an ailing economy after the financial crisis of 2008. Prior to that, an owner who wanted to retire could sell their business to a competitor or to a private equity firm in a leveraged buyout transaction. After the crisis, this was no longer an option as most potential acquirers were short of cash. Selling the business to employees via an ESOP became a logical way forward.

The position of ESOPs was further consolidated in 2022, when Congress passed a bill requiring the US Department of Labor to: 1) establish within the Employment and Training Administration an initiative to promote employee ownership and participation in business decision-making; and 2) introduce grants for outreach, technical assistance and training to encourage new and existing state programmes to foster employee ownership and participation in business decision-making.[6]

The relation between employee ownership policies and economic crisis is an interesting one: the last time ESOPs were given a boost in the US was through the Tax Reform Act of 1984, introduced largely in response to the oil crisis of the previous decade. The pattern is all too familiar. In moments of crisis, the free market consistently turns to the public as its saviour. Like Margaret Thatcher's right-to-buy scheme, introduced in the 1980 UK Housing Act, the 1984 US Tax Reform Act can be interpreted as an effort to mobilize mass participation in the financial system in order to save the system from itself. The same could be said of the promotion of self-building as a form of home provision in the Netherlands following the 2008 financial crisis. In times of crisis, irrespective of the political complexion of those in power, the organized unfolding of the free market remains suspiciously reliant on socialist models.

ꝏ

Since the introduction of the EOT in 2014, employee ownership in the UK has grown by 90 per cent. There are currently more than 2,200 employee-owned businesses nationally, a rise of over 25 per cent since 2024.[7] However, given that there are roughly 5.6 million businesses in the UK,[8] the overall percentage is still minuscule. The situation is similar in the US, with even smaller numbers.

One sector where the idea has gained above-average traction is the architecture profession. As of 2019, 20 per cent of the largest 100 architecture firms in the UK are employee-owned.[9] To name a few: Cullinan Studio, established as a cooperative in 1981; Make, established in 2004; and, more recently, Page\Park (2013), Architype (2015), Stride Treglown (2015), ADP (2017), Allford Hall Monaghan Morris (2017), Anderson Bell + Christie (2017), Assael (2019), Buckley Gray Yeoman (2019), Haworth Tompkins (2019), Lovelock Mitchell Architects (2019), Triangle Architects (2019), Studio Egret West (2020), Hawkins\Brown (2021), HLM Architects (2021), LDA (2021), Purcell (2021), and the UK's largest employee-owned firm, Zaha Hadid Architects (2022).

There has been a similar trend elsewhere in the English-speaking world. In the US, HDR has been employee-owned since 1996, followed more recently by IA Interior Architects (2014), Taylor Design (2018), SHoP (2021) and BNIM (2023). In Canada there are JLR, RRM, Parkin and NORR, in Australia i2C and Meld Studios, and in New Zealand Boffa Miskell.

By far the largest employee-owned architecture firm in the world to date is the US company Gensler. It has retained that status ever since its transition in 1989, which largely came about because of the 1984 US Tax Reform Act. In Gensler's case, employee ownership is no small matter: in 2023, the company employed a total of 6,000 people and generated $1.78 billion in revenue.[10] These figures stand in stark contrast to the firm's humble beginnings: M. Arthur Gensler Jr. & Associates was founded in 1965 in a one-room storefront at 555 Clay Street, San Francisco, as a husband-and-wife practice with limited funds in the bank and four kids to feed at home. One might say that Arthur (Art) and Drucilla (Drue) Gensler represent the American Dream in every way.

An intriguing feature of Gensler is how it has managed to retain anonymity despite its size. Almost every architect will know the firm, but most would struggle to name one of its projects. Its website typically shows interior work and not the eye-catching or 'iconic' projects one might expect from such a large firm. Rather than having an architectural mission, Gensler seems to be the product of business acumen, as was evidenced in its early approach to getting work. The firm's first projects focused on tenant-improvement work. From there, its portfolio gradually expanded into office interiors – a well-calculated move, since most office buildings in the US at the time were designed as core and shell. Interior design, which could include anything from high-quality interior finishes to increased ceiling heights and upgraded restroom and elevator lobbies, represented an entirely new niche – a need the market didn't know it had but soon came to devour.

Under the direction of its main client, Houston-based developer Gregory Hines, Gensler developed what has come to be known as 'a trickle-down high-design strategy' – the design of bespoke office interiors with the express aim of setting a standard for tenants to follow. The avalanche of commissions that followed accelerated the growth of the firm in subsequent decades. Growth implied continuity, and continuity implied succession planning. The firm had more or less operated as a family business since 1965, but in 1989 it transitioned to an employee-owned entity. A board of directors and an executive committee were instated in 2000, formalizing a collaborative leadership structure that now extends to studios, offices, regions, practice areas and design disciplines.[11]

Key to maintaining this corporate structure is the grooming of future generations. In 2004, the firm set up an in-house system of education, referred to as 'Gensler University'. In 2007, it launched the Gensler Research Program (now called the Gensler Research Institute) with the goal of 'developing a deeper understanding of the connection between design, business, and the human experience'. Falling under the Program's aegis are workplace surveys, the Workplace Performance Index, a formalized review process, three volumes of research catalogues detailing case studies, and ultimately research into all practice areas. More than the work, Gensler's ultimate capital is its workers, even if the firm itself may stop well short of ever calling them such.

Gensler is routinely frowned upon by the architecture community. This might be the architecture community's loss rather than Gensler's. For all its nondescript work, staged anonymity and corporate rituals, it can be argued that Gensler in its present form represents the most advanced state in the evolution of architecture as a practice: the evolution into business. Gensler is the largest and most prominent firm in the world to recognize the importance not of works of architecture, but of the work of architects.

Thinking of architecture as business is a comparatively recent phenomenon. Before the Renaissance, architecture was not a recognized profession. Unlike the painter or sculptor, the designer of buildings did not have a clearly defined place within the trades. There was no standard training for those wishing to practise architecture, and no guild devoted specifically to the professional interests of architects. The men who made the plans for churches and palaces were ranked alongside humble artisans.

Architects were trained through an apprenticeship system. Work and education coincided; no employment relation existed in the strict sense. Apprentices provided their labour in exchange for the training needed either to succeed their masters or set out on their own. This tradition continued until well after the system of apprenticeship had been dismantled: Brancusi worked for Rodin, Le Corbusier for Perret, Frank Lloyd Wright for Louis Sullivan.

The architecture profession as we know it today largely emerged in the nineteenth century, when the protection of the title was initiated, a licensing system came into being and architects were taught their trade at accredited schools and universities. The profession of the architect counted as one of the liberal professions: a category that typically involves providing specialized services based on intellectual or artistic expertise, usually characterized by a high degree of autonomy and carried out by individuals or small partnerships (as with doctors, lawyers or accountants).

One of the first architecture offices to employ large numbers of workers was that of George Gilbert Scott in London (established in 1833), with some 800 architects and draughtsmen on the payroll. His example was later followed in Chicago in 1867 by William Le Baron Jenney, designer of the Home Insurance Building in the same city. Among the architects employed there were Daniel Burnham and Louis Sullivan.

It was Chicago in particular, a city in the grip of an unprecedented building boom at the time, that revolutionized not only the construction industry but also the practice of architecture. Louis Sullivan rose to fame largely thanks to that building boom. His firm, Adler & Sullivan, worked on more than 250 projects between 1883 and 1894. Their main competitor, Burnham and Root (1873), was the largest architecture firm in the world at the time of Burnham's death in 1912. Continued as Graham, Anderson, Probst & White (GAP&W), it retained that status throughout the first half of the twentieth century. It was firms like these which, for the first time, offered the possibility of pursuing architecture as a corporate career, with 'having one's name on the door' as the ultimate reward.

The late-nineteenth-century Chicago building boom, and the subsequent reinvention of architecture as business, paved the way for big corporate adventures in the twentieth century: Louis Skidmore and Nathaniel Owings launched their firm in 1936, joined by John Merrill three years later; George F. Hellmuth, Gyo Obata and George Kassabaum, three young graduates of the School of Architecture at Washington University in St Louis, founded their own company in 1955; and A. Eugene Kohn, William Pedersen and Sheldon Fox set up theirs in 1976.

The names of these architects may have faded into the background with time, but today the firms they launched are the brands of choice for corporate clients, with a global reach and portfolios to match. Like the large Chicago firms of the late nineteenth century, these three are businesses first and foremost, a product of the economies whose waves they rode: the economic tailwind of postwar America; the oil boom of the Middle East in the 1960s; the surge of the Asian tigers in the 1970s and '80s, culminating in an opened-up China since the end of the millennium.

SOM, HOK, KPF: three-letter acronyms, formed from the initials of men nobody remembers, whose reputations have been eclipsed by that of the firms they started. Nathaniel Owings was the last of SOM's three name partners to die (in 1984). Generations of partners have since come and gone. Worthy of note: Gordon Bunshaft, the only architect at the firm whose name has left a lasting imprint, was never more than an employee.

All for the better perhaps. The prominence of founders tends to complicate business in the long run. From vocation to occupation; from occupation to profession; from profession to business – with all the associated and necessary anonymity. No longer is it relevant to have one's name on the door. In the last stage of the evolution of architecture, names are the first casualty. Ultimately, capitalism is agnostic towards individuals. Again: individuals are mortal, businesses ought not to be. For the time being, the best way to ensure that is to enlist all the individuals involved. Collective Architecture, Hawkins\Brown, Gensler, Zaha Hadid Architects . . . After partnerships, employee ownership is now the model of choice for continuity and growth.

The Nuttall Review had its tenth anniversary in 2022 – long enough to evaluate its consequences. As indeed happened, in the form of a new report: 'Celebrating the 10th anniversary of the Nuttall Review'. The main source of evaluation of the

Nuttall Review has been its own sequel, the conclusions of which – and this may come as no surprise – are positive. The UK has rallied around the idea, celebrating 'Employment Ownership Day' in June (the month the Nuttall Review was first presented) every year.

Not so positive is some of the independent feedback. Will Stephens, communications coordinator at United Voices of the World – Section of Architectural Workers ('End unpaid overtime; pay living wages!'), states that: 'Employee-owned trusts do not really divest power from business-owners to their employees as the owners choose the way it is set up . . . This will not lead to the redress of power that we believe is needed in the architectural industry.'[12]

So far, the model primarily seems to be one for retirement and succession, with little or no effect on the day-to-day work – merely a form of window dressing according to some, and a far cry from the idealism of the early pioneers. In 1978, Ted Cullinan, figurehead of the UK's first collectively owned architect practice, wrote a one-page manifesto arguing that 'design and building of necessity involves co-operation'. It begins: 'The design of buildings is a social act. If it is to reflect concern with progressive social relations and hope for the future, it seems important to us that the social and financial organisation of the group should match that concern as far as possible.' Further on he states: 'The Architect-master and his servants co-operate as do employees of corporate or state design organisations; but one is distorted by individual possession and the other by rule and anonymity.' His own firm (for some reason still called Cullinan Studio) serves as evidence:

> For eight years now we have found that the special contributions of eight individuals find best combined expression when the co-operative idea is paramount, supported by shared concern with the quality of the work that we do, as well as the will to share it and the money. Fees are shared in agreed proportions as and when they are received; any surplus is shared out or used otherwise by agreement. Making the practice have no book value ensures that it is no one's possession nor is anyone its servant.[13]

The prose is considerably more militant than that of the Nuttall Review. And Cullinan was in good company. Before him, radical supergroups of the 1960s, like Archigram (1960, London), Archizoom and Superstudio (Florence, 1966), Ant Farm (San Francisco, 1968) and Haus-Rucker-Co (Vienna, 1967), had acted as collectives. Since then, there have been Memphis Group (Milan, 1980), Matrix (London, 1981), NATØ (London, 1983) and Raumlabor (Berlin, 1999).

The idea has survived into the new century too, with architects' collectives popping up all over Europe. In no particular order: Zuloark (Madrid, 2001), Exyzt (Paris, 2002), baukuh (Milan, 2004), Lacol (Barcelona, 2009), Assemble (London, Bristol, 2010), A-A Collective (Basel, Copenhagen, Warsaw, Milano, 2010), Collectif Etc (Marseille, 2010), orizzontale (Rome, 2010), n'UNDO (Madrid, 2011), Warehouse (Lisbon, 2013), CNCRT (Bari, Paris, Zurich, 2014), false mirror office (Brussels, Florence, Genoa, Lausanne, Paris, 2015), Fosbury Architecture (Milan, 2013), X=(T=E=N) (Zurich, Belgrade, 2018), la-clique (Lausanne, 2019), Trojans Collective (Geneva, 2019).

The appeal of the collective practice seems to be unrelenting. In the words of Marson Korbi of CNCRT: 'The possibility of a counter architecture, or an architecture outside the system or an alternative to the system, was very much part of Raumlabor's beginnings . . . Twenty years later, the question is still valid: to what extent can we, inside the capitalist reproductive system, offer any kind of counter system?'[14]

Notwithstanding the revolutionary zeal of such statements, most of the earlier collectives either dissolved with the death of their founders or have continued in some permanently experimental state. Even the early momentum of a practice like Assemble seems to have withered away. Inventing a plausible alternative for practice – a truly collective working model beyond the mere divesting of financial risks – remains a sticky affair. The more collective the work process we aspire to, the greater the marginality to which we seem to be condemned. Work is both a verb and a noun, yet all too often it seems that we are forced to choose between the two.

No art without suffering – so it is commonly believed. But while the presentation of Collective Architecture offered abundant proof of that cliché, it also leaves us with an unwavering desire to move beyond. Does the real and obvious utopia not emerge from taking equally seriously the antonym – no suffering without art? To what extent do artistic pretentions offer a lazy pretext for maintaining an imperfect and unfair system of relations? Is it too much to expect a 'best of both worlds'? Can mind-blowing buildings emerge from radically fair conditions? There is only one way to find out: collectivize practice, effective immediately!

4

Time's Up!

I have little time left. I no longer travel, so as to be free to devote myself to my family and friends. However, I still go to my office in Copacabana every day from nine in the morning to seven in the evening, Saturdays included. I am incapable of sitting in an armchair doing nothing or simply brooding over the miseries of existence. For me, architecture has always been a hobby as well as a profession; it attracts and absorbs me, but I don't attach much importance to it. The main thing for me is to feel at ease with myself, to remain on the side of the needy and to denounce social injustices. That said, I have acquired a certain renown and the commissions still flow in. I have, however, reduced my team to four people so as to have a quieter life. It is important to remain active right up to the end. You only live once.[1]

The time left proved to be anything but little. He would live to be 104 and go on to practise for another twenty years: Oscar

Ribeiro de Almeida Niemeyer Soares Filho – O.N. to his friends – one of the most prolific architects of the twentieth century.

While the length of Niemeyer's career may be exceptional, it is symptomatic of how architecture offers its practitioners a longer career than most other professions. For architects, retirement is an anathema, often synonymous with death. Niemeyer's productive life equals that of three to four generations (which may well explain why Brazil has not produced a famous architect since).

At the time of this interview, in 1992, Niemeyer's oeuvre boasted an impressive seventy-three completed buildings, and that number had increased to well over 100 by the time of his death in 2012.

His projects are too many to list; they include private residences, university buildings, museums, the French Communist Party Headquarters, the Algiers Mosque, the Mondadori publishing company headquarters, the Latin America Memorial, the Serpentine Gallery Pavilion, and a museum in Curitiba named after himself. But more than anything, his name will forever be associated with the city he helped imagine and shape. Brasília, the new and shiny capital of his country of birth, was the testing ground for his very own mutant brand of twentieth-century modernism, a brand celebrated, vilified, discarded, forgotten, rediscovered and then cautiously celebrated again.

The same could be said of Niemeyer himself. The highs and lows of his career exemplify in the extreme the meandering trajectory that a successful architect is destined to travel. His life was tainted by fate more than once. It was in a hotel room in Lisbon, listening to the radio, that he first heard of the 1964 putsch. Brazil's elected left-wing government had been overthrown by the military, in a coup backed by the United States. The country's constitution of 1946 was suspended and a new government, headed by Brazil's army chief of staff, granted itself unlimited powers to remove elected officials, dismiss civil servants and revoke the political rights of those suspected of any kind of subversion.

On the day of his return, Niemeyer, a lifelong communist activist, was interrogated by the army. His studio had been ransacked, as had the office of *Módulo*, the architecture magazine he had helped start. No immediate measures were taken to limit his capacity to practise, but the political pressure against him steadily grew. His new circular terminal, approved earlier for Brasília's airport, was rejected without further explanation; his Júlia Kubitschek School was demolished. The fateful moment came while he was working on the Ministry of the Army building in Brasília, when the officer in charge warned him that he was about to be arrested for offering financial assistance to people hiding from the regime.

He left for Israel. What was intended to be a short visit to discuss potential projects (for the Dan Hotel chain) became a stay of six months, during which he designed massive high-rise projects for Tel Aviv, Haifa and the Negev. He left Israel for France, where he set up a studio in Paris with the help of André Malraux. Most of Niemeyer's built legacy on this side of the Atlantic was conceived there, such as the headquarters for Mondadori, the Fata Engineering headquarters in Italy, the University of Constantine, the dome of the Olympic arena in Algeria and, of course, the headquarters of the French Communist Party in Paris itself.

Niemeyer continued to operate from France until the mid-1980s. In Brazil, after a transition to civilian rule had been agreed to by the military (a promise made in the late 1970s), elections were held on 15 January 1985, and José Sarney of the centrist Brazilian Democratic Movement assumed the presidency. After a twenty-one-year exile, Niemeyer was finally able to return home. Three years later, he was awarded the Pritzker Prize for his life's work, at the respectable age of eighty-one.

If there is one life of an architect that cries out to be turned into a screenplay, it is probably Niemeyer's. Its episodes unfold along the plotlines of a Hollywood drama: a promising beginning cut short by fate; a personal struggle to overcome; triumph despite the odds; followed by a belated recognition by the world at large. It is the path of Howard Roark in *The Fountainhead*. In real life, it was the path of Wright, Corb, Mies or any other twentieth-century architect of reverence.

Yet, something is different with Niemeyer. Not so much due to the nature of his career itself, its culmination, or the path it took to get there, but rather because of what happened after. Niemeyer was indeed one of the most prolific architects of the twentieth century, but he may also be one of the most prolific of the twenty-first. He continued working well after having received the Pritzker. What should have been a modest epilogue evolved into an infinitely prolonged afterlife – longer than the period he lived in exile, longer even than the period leading up to it. Niemeyer after Niemeyer exceeds Niemeyer.

Largely because of that, it has become impossible to dismiss Niemeyer as a product of his time. What time? He is his own before and after. Even if his work is characterized by a remarkable consistency, its never-ending nature has come to inspire a perpetual form of progressive insight about the work itself. The late Niemeyer openly reveals the implicit message of the early

Niemeyer. It is because of the later work that we recognize the earlier as having also consistently gone against the grain.

If the principle of twentieth-century architecture was that form follows function, Niemeyer's work never complied. More than machines to produce well-functioning spaces, his buildings are a form of expressionism and, as such, emphatically irrational. Historically, the late Niemeyer might simply be interpreted as a postmodern iteration of the early Niemeyer. And perhaps that is what he always was – a postmodernist, someone who understood, before anyone else, that modernism could be practised as a form of mannerism, that it carried within itself the potential for a second lease of life as the antithesis of everything it professed to be.

The same applies to Niemeyer's political convictions – a curious mix of sincerity and style, at once apolitical and hyperpolitical. In an interview with *Metropolis* in 2006, when asked about the ability of his architecture to improve the quality of life and bring rich and poor together, he replied: 'No, just like any architecture, mine doesn't help it at all. Architecture has always been directed to the upper class, and things haven't changed.' Asked if he would change anything about Brasília, his reply was simply: 'Not at all. I think it is okay like it is.' He even candidly admitted that personally he preferred to live in Rio de Janeiro: 'I want the beach, the mountains, the chaos; I want Rio.'[2]

With age there inevitably comes an increasing awareness of the limitations of one's profession – of its ability to change society, the world, or anything at all for that matter. To read into Niemeyer's answers any kind of political indifference, however, would be misguided. When asked about the house he built for his personal driver in a Rio favela, his reply was unmistakably political:

> He is a Brazilian man, a poor man, one who was born poor and will die poor. Of course, his life improved with his new house, but this is an exception. Housing is always the beginning of any change in someone's life. One needs to have a worthy place to live, and the state should provide it to everybody. But I insist that the answer to this change is not architecture. It is revolution.[3]

A personal friend of Fidel Castro, Niemeyer might have thought it wise to downplay the political importance of architecture. In the context of a socialist revolution, the relevance of buildings is reduced to the organized provision of space for those who need it. Pondering on their larger significance is no more than a bourgeois pastime. The only plausible response to Le Corbusier's 'architecture or revolution' is that there is no 'or'; they exist simultaneously – architecture *and* revolution – sometimes in tandem, more often independently. In Niemeyer's universe, ideology and expression have an incidental relation at most.

Nothing lasts forever and neither did Niemeyer's untouchable status. Serious doubts had been entertained about the ongoing relevance of his architecture long before his death in 2012. His laureation for the Pritzker Prize in 1988 – shared with Gordon Bunshaft – was met with a mix of surprise and scepticism. In the *New York Times*, Paul Goldberger argued that, by choosing Niemeyer and Bunshaft, the jury could not have found two architects who better represented the antithesis of the values of the time:

> True, Mr. Bunshaft and Mr. Niemeyer are deeply committed to the pursuit of architecture as an art. But they are also

> essentially indifferent to values that have become important in the last generation – that buildings should relate to the physical and cultural makeup of the place in which they are built. Mr. Bunshaft and Mr. Niemeyer have tended, in spite of rhetoric about social needs, to design buildings that are pure objects first, cultural presences second.[4]

Given what we know today, Goldberger's concluding statement that 'the nomination of two men averaging an age of 80 must be interpreted as a message about the present state of architecture', acquires an interesting twist. While Bunshaft died two years later, Niemeyer would continue to practise for almost a quarter of a century. In 1988, Niemeyer *was* the present state of architecture – not at the end, but in the middle of his career.

Further awards followed. Lots of them. In 1990, notwithstanding the fact that he was an atheist, Niemeyer was made Knight Commander of the Order of St Gregory the Great by Pope John Paul II; in 1998, aged ninety-one, he was awarded the RIBA Royal Gold Medal; in 2000, he published his memoirs, *The Curves of Time*, only to embark on another victory lap; in 2003, at ninety-six, he was called upon to design the Serpentine Pavilion; in 2004, he was awarded the Praemium Imperiale; in 2007, he received the Legion d'honneur.

But if the awarding of the Pritzker Prize led to some raised eyebrows, it was his last award, the Order of Friendship given to him by Russia's President Vladimir Putin for his 100th birthday, that definitively landed him on the wrong side of history – in the company of faded celebrities such as Gerard Depardieu and Bernie Ecclestone. Increasingly, questions were being asked about the abilities of a century-old architect. What, beyond an endless tribute to the past, to times supposedly more adventurous and challenging than our own, could possibly be the significance of Niemeyer in a world that had dispensed both with his political ideology – a communist after the fall of the Berlin Wall – and with his type of architecture – a modernist after the Strada Novissima?

In 2007 in the *New York Times*, reviewing Niemeyer's latest work in Brasília, Nicolai Ouroussoff openly wondered if the architect shouldn't be protected against himself:

> It is not simply that his latest buildings have a careless, tossed-off quality. It's that some of his most revered buildings, from the Brasília Cathedral to the grand Monumental Axis of the city itself, have been marred by the architect's own hand. And this poses an uncomfortable dilemma: At what point do we, that is, the public that idolizes him, his government and private clients, have an obligation to intervene? Or is posing the question an act of spectacularly bad taste?[5]

Ouroussoff's observations did not stop at the Cathedral or the grand Axis:

> In the mid-1980s, Mr. Niemeyer altered the shape of the arches that frame the main facade of his Ministry of Justice building, sacrificing the elegance of their symmetry in favor of something more whimsical. Mr. Niemeyer painted its exposed concrete structure white, and he replaced its towering windows with stained-glass panels: changes that detract from the raw force of the building's upward thrust.

From these individual points of critique, it is a small step to a general conclusion:

> To those who pay close attention, the decline in the quality of Niemeyer's work, whether resulting from a creative lull or complacency brought on by fame or old age, has been evident since he completed his Museum of Contemporary Art in Niteroi in 1996 . . . It's as if the museum were designed by a lesser talent who could mimic the graceful lines in Mr. Niemeyer's sketches but lacked the skill and patience to see the design through.

But most lethal of all are Ouroussoff's last words:

> Nobody can fault Mr. Niemeyer for his desire to keep working; that his enthusiasm is undimmed at the age of 100 is cause for awe. And it's laudable that he approaches his past work without an exaggerated self-importance. Cities are not museum pieces; without constant change, they lose their cultural vitality. Yet the value of these Modernist buildings as part of our shared cultural memory, the foundation of our identity, cannot be underestimated.

Niemeyer had just been officially identified as his own worst enemy.

There was more negativity, and not just from architecture critics. In 2007, Niemeyer's aquatic centre project in Potsdam, Germany – a series of separate pools surrounded by a glass gallery with a controlled microclimate – saw its funding cut off for fear of going over budget. 'Good for Brazil, not for Potsdam', according to the contractor.[6] In the words of the centre's manager: 'Even operating this pool would also have been expensive, . . . everything was very far apart, spread out over the mountain . . . We would have had to have supervisors in each of the many pool areas.' His acknowledgement of the project's architectural qualities ends up being no more than a byline: 'But it would have been an eye-catcher.'[7]

The project was subsequently given to GMP.

If Niemeyer's work itself had become increasingly anachronistic, positively senile was his ongoing tribute to the female form – the only apparent rationale behind his increasingly flamboyant designs. 'My work is not about form follows function', he would say, 'but about "form follows feminine" . . . I am not attracted to straight angles or to the straight line, hard and inflexible, created by man, I am attracted to free-flowing sensual curves. The curves that I find in the mountains of my country, in the sinuousness of its rivers, in the waves of the ocean, and on the body of the beloved woman.'[8]

The inspiration adorned the interior of his studio, in the middle of which, set up like a mini classroom, three rows of stadium seats faced an easel with one of his own paintings – of a voluptuous long-haired woman on horseback. While once a source of amusement among architecture critics, this uninhibited display of enthusiasm for the opposite sex would soon meet with a very different sort of response, though not quite in Niemeyer's lifetime. In a 2012 obituary in the *Guardian*, Oliver Wainwright mused on the way one of Niemeyer's friends reminisced about a party welcoming foreign architects in Brasília: 'None of your snooty cocktail parties, when a man wants a party, he needs a woman. Let's call up a few girls.'[9] One wonders if Wainwright would entertain the same musings today.

A few other quotes from the same source:

> Crude line drawings of such beloved women – variously cavorting, supine, or half-merging into a building – adorn the pages of his memoirs, The Curves of Time, which provide a fascinating insight into the man behind the monuments . . . It is this mischievous sense of fun and delight that will live on in the buildings of Oscar Niemeyer. He brought a much-needed injection of passion and emotion to the monotonous world of modernism, an outlook that lifted the spirits and continues to have a lasting legacy.

Niemeyer's first wife died in 2004. In 2006 he married his secretary, Vera Lucia Cabreira, a woman, even at sixty, forty years his junior. 'Life without women is pointless', he once said.[10]

Niemeyer kept working on the design of buildings right up until his death in 2012, visiting his office daily, shuttled back and forth from his home by his driver, arriving at work at 9:30 every morning and staying until well into the evening, often even on weekends.

While the rest of the world might have been questioning the use of in-situ concrete for quite some time – time-consuming in construction and hard to justify in environmental terms – not so Niemeyer. His last years were spent pretty much in the same way as all the many years before: conjuring up modernist masterpieces, curved (of course), gravity defying, stretching the possibilities of reinforced concrete to yet more unimaginable extremes. In 2009, while hospitalized for four weeks for the treatment of gallstones and an intestinal tumour, he was quoted as saying: 'I need to keep busy, keep in touch with friends, maintain my rhythm of life.'[11]

And he did. Released from hospital, he managed to complete the designs for another six buildings: Centro Administrativo Presidente Tancredo Neves (Belo Horizonte, 2010), Oscar Niemeyer International Cultural Centre (Avilés, 2011), Tribunal Superior Eleitoral (Brasília, 2011), Oscar Niemeyer Auditorium (Ravello, Italy, 2011), Brasília Digital TV Tower (2012), Museum of Popular Arts of Paraíba (2012).

Niemeyer eventually died on 5 December 2012, at the Hospital Samaritano in Rio de Janeiro, of cardiorespiratory arrest, 104 years of age.

Niemeyer has enjoyed a revival in popularity in recent times. An article Michael Kimmelman wrote about him in the *New York Times*, after visiting him in his office, reads like an early eulogy:

> A suave pioneer of curvaceous concrete, toying with the limits of engineering while injecting sex and surrealism into Le Corbusier's famous machine for living, authoring some of the most audacious, sublimely poetic and occasionally goofy buildings of the twentieth century, bringing, more than anyone else, lyricism and a populist sensibility to modern architecture.[12]

The enduring admiration (including my own) for Niemeyer as an architect makes him a tricky example for the case I'm trying to argue. In a certain sense, his career is at once an argument *for* and *against* retirement. Much of his life and work will go down in history as distinctly out of touch with reality. At the same time, his carefully cultivated disregard for the Zeitgeist serves as proof that, if you live long enough, you inevitably become 'of the times' again, if only as a quaint old relic.

His effect on architecture in Brazil has been double-edged. Just as Finland continues to be impaired by the legacy of Alvar Aalto, Brazil is hampered by that of Niemeyer. Both architects have had the effect of 'vacuum bombs' on their respective contexts. Niemeyer may be a national hero, but hardly a Brazilian architect of note has emerged after him. One wonders how many talents could have thrived, but never did because of his long shadow? The Brazilian architecture scene is one of nostalgia for bygone days – days which may never have existed in the way they are currently remembered.

Niemeyer may be an extreme case, but it is a general truth that careers in architecture far outlast those of other professions. There are good reasons for that. Architecture is a slow profession. It can take years, sometimes decades, to complete a building project. Moreover, it takes (built) work to acquire work. Building a substantial enough portfolio to receive any sort of prestigious commission can take a lifetime, or at least a working lifetime. Most architects produce their magnum opus at a late stage in life, often well beyond what in most professions would be considered retirement age.

Louis Kahn was sixty-four when he completed the Salk Institute for Biological Studies; Mies van der Rohe was sixty-five when he completed the Farnsworth House; Álvaro Siza was sixty-six when he completed the Serralves Museum of Contemporary Art; Peter Cook was sixty-seven when he built Kunsthaus Graz (and eighty when he completed his first building in the UK); Frank Gehry was sixty-eight when he completed Guggenheim Bilbao; Rafael Viñoly was seventy-one when he completed 432 Park Avenue; I. M. Pei was seventy-one when he completed the Louvre Pyramid. Cesar Pelli was seventy-two when he completed the Petronas Towers; Frank Lloyd Wright was ninety-one when he completed the Guggenheim Museum. He died the same year.

Things haven't really changed. Some of today's best-known architects started practising as early as the 1960s and are currently in their eighties. The emergence of mass media helped propel them to great fame. Architects got to be celebrated as rock stars. Major prizes, like the Pritzker, the RIBA Gold Medal and the AIA awards, overwhelmingly go to the most established names. They control institutions, architecture schools and award committees. Despite being only one partner in a large firm, which they often co-own with younger partners, many of them continue to be regarded as the sole proprietor of the work.

It is this limited group of architects that gets to define what is 'innovative', often bending that definition to suit their own legacy, regarding themselves as radical visionaries even when their work, like Niemeyer's, has become highly derivative of past successes. Futile style variations serve to mask utter stagnation in terms of substance. What ensues is an endless, self-perpetuating cycle of pseudo innovations – disruptive enough to get noticed, safe enough to never really disrupt anything.

The belief that great architects only get better with age and remain forever at the cutting edge creates a vicious cycle. Major projects invariably go to established names. Younger architects working for them spend years learning how to refine and reproduce the work of their seniors. By the time they reach their own peak, they have internalized the same conservatism, creating a cycle in which 'radical' becomes synonymous with incremental changes to the old masters' ideas. It is telling that any architect under forty-five can qualify as an 'emerging architect'.

It all begs the question: is the ongoing presence of old architects the symptom of an industry that is inherently slow-moving, or is the industry slow-moving because of the ongoing presence of old architects?

It's entirely possible – and arguably quite likely – that the average age of the leading architects is itself a cause of stagnation and conservatism, rather than just a consequence of the profession's inherent nature. In other words, rather than the slow-moving nature of architecture necessitating older leadership, the entrenchment of older architects at the top is what makes the industry slow-moving in the first place.

Old architects have shaped the system to ensure their own continued dominance, reinforcing a false narrative that only they are capable of radical innovation. The building industry stands on the brink of seismic changes. Off-site manufacturing, 3D printing and robotics, AI and digital-twin technology – all could cause massive disruptions in how we design, build and manage projects over the next decade. How much longer will we continue to pin our hopes on 'radical' old men claiming to reinvent the wheel every decade?

Apple was able to outlive Steve Jobs; Microsoft has moved on from Bill Gates. Even the Trump brand has survived its name-giver being preoccupied with other things. Whether it is a matter of architects not wanting to retire or not being in a position to do so is often deflected as a chicken and egg question. More likely, the two are inextricably linked. The common age of retirement for most professions globally is sixty-seven. It is time that architects stopped regarding themselves as an exception. Our profession is being held hostage to heroes well beyond their expiry date. It is time they make way.

At the time of writing: Frank Gehry – 96 years (1929); Denise Scott Brown – 94 years (1931); Peter Eisenman – 93 years (1932); Herman Hertzberger – 93 years (1932); Alvaro Siza – 92 years (1933); Richard Meier – 91 years (1934) (retired in 2018 because of #MeToo); Norman Foster – 90 years (1935); Glenn Murcutt – 89 years (1936); Peter Cook – 89 years (1936); Rafael Moneo – 88 years (1937); Renzo Piano – 88 years (1937); Moshe Safdie – 87 years (1938); Robert A. M. Stern – 86 years (1939); Nicholas Grimshaw – 86 years (1939); Tadao Ando – 84 years (1941); Toyo Ito – 84 years (1941); Wolf Dieter Prix – 84 years (1941); Mario Botta – 82 years (1943); Peter Zumthor – 82 years (1943); Eric Owen Moss – 82 years (1943); Christian de Portzamparc – 81 years (1944); Bernard Tschumi – 81 years (1944); Thom Mayne – 81 years (1944); Massimiliano Fuksas – 81 years (1944); Rem Koolhaas – 81 years (1944); Jean Nouvel – 80 years (1945); Léon Krier – 79 years (1946); Daniel Libeskind – 79 years (1946); Alberto Campo Baeza – 79 years (1946); Hans Kollhoff – 79 years (1946); Steven Holl – 78 years (1947); Pierre de Meuron – 75 years (1950); Jacques Herzog – 75 years (1950); Santiago Calatrava – 74 years (1951); Dominique Perrault – 72 years (1953); David Chipperfield – 72 years (1953); Kengo Kuma – 71 years (1954); Stefano Boeri – 69 years (1956); Kazuyo Sejima – 69 years (1956); Shigeru Ban – 68 years (1957); Elizabeth Diller – 67 years (1958).

5

Free for All

'NO!' The answer is remarkably short given the lengthy exchange that led up to it, which hardly anyone in the room has been able to understand. Japanese is a language off-limits for most.

I look on with envy, marvelling at the effectiveness of a strategy which involves no facts, figures, dialogue, interactivity, negotiation, persuasion or even basic communication skills. A simple, two-letter word has just rendered all the unwritten rules of engagement moot.

The client seems baffled. Where do we go from here? The abrupt reply rules out any possibility of this being a 'lost in translation' problem. There is no point in asking the same question again. The translator has put the request to the architect, who has listened attentively, asked for further clarification (at least, that is what we guess she did), after which the translator has once again conveyed the client's appeal. The architect looks at her translator with apparent disbelief. After an extensive back and forth – allegedly the translator is an architect too – they render their verdict, succinctly and decisively. Obviously, this is a precarious situation. Politesse is of the essence – Japanese too – but what diplomatic reply is there to a question that ought not be asked?

Would she be prepared to lower the height of the building she has proposed: a 180-metre-high glass dome measuring 360 metres in diameter? Would she, purely for cost reasons, consider lowering the dome to, let's say, 150 metres? If she insists on maintaining the same proportions – the dome is half a sphere – she is welcome to apply the same reduction in plan. The client has indicated he is more than willing to accept the attendant reduction in square metres. Same building, smaller size.

The latter should be an easy concession. The Dome doesn't really have a brief. At least, no brief in the way building briefs are normally defined, in the form of a (set of) prescribed use(s), square metres, gross to net ratios, net lettable space, and so on. Instead, the Dome is loosely defined as an 'arrival experience'. It is the entry point to a larger area labelled the 'Guest Zone', the imagined centre of a newly planned science campus on the outskirts of Moscow. Apart from some shrubbery, intersected by a few winding paths and some portacabin toilet units, there is nothing much the Dome covers. Its purpose is to offer relief from the extreme winter cold and the ever higher summer temperatures. It is there to be 'a place of refuge' from the harsh Russian climate – all 100,000 square metres of it.

The same lack of definition that plagues the Dome and the Guest Zone plagues the campus as a whole. It is unclear for whom, or for what sciences, the science campus is being developed. Throughout the process, there has been no hint as to what kind of businesses or what fields of expertise the initiative is targeting. Famous architects have been invited to contribute, but they seem to be there mostly to raise the profile of a project that refuses to take on a profile otherwise. They are expected to sign up and endorse the initiative, whatever the initiative is.

That poses a few problems. In the absence of a clear brief, the architects have decided to write their own. During a hastily organized dinner – the invitation to which never reached the client – they have carved up the Guest Zone into separate sections allowing each of them to do their own thing. What better way of signing up to the project than with a forthright delivery of their signature brand of architecture? As an architectural stunt, the Dome is just one of many. (The author of this book worked on a building called 'The Rock'.) Subdivision of the land eliminates all need for coordination or dialogue. Each architect is given carte blanche, accountable only to their self-formulated brief, the text of which they can change at will. The function of the buildings is whatever the architects say it should be. The buildings themselves are good when they are happy with them. Surrendered up to their collective aspirations, the Guest Zone becomes a self-fulfilling architectural nirvana, in which each architect acts as judge, jury, prosecution and defence of their own project. The client is but a witness, resigned to the role of benevolent sponsor. Call it facilitation.

'No part of this work may be altered, adapted or modified in any form without the prior written consent of the author . . .' The 'moral rights of the author' – as laws concerning intellectual property commonly phrase it – also pertain to works of architecture. As such, the preceding anecdote is not an anomaly. The work of architects is generally put on a par with that of writers, poets, painters and musicians, in line with the prevailing view that, like works of literature, art and music, works of architecture are an expression of the personality of their author. Thus, they are unique to the author and non-transferable. The moral rights of authors include the right to object to any distortion or mutilation of the original work which would be prejudicial to the author's honour or reputation.[1] And that, in fact, was exactly the right that the Japanese architect (the author) exercised in relation to her dome (the original work).

There is only one problem. The proposed dome hardly qualified as an original work. A similar dome had been proposed by Richard Buckminster Fuller fifty years earlier for the US Pavilion at Expo 67 in Montreal. Like the Japanese architect's dome, Fuller's dome too had been conceived as a 'biosphere' – a conditioned environment with an autonomous microclimate independent of the world outside. The Montreal dome itself had a precursor in the giant dome Fuller had proposed to place over Manhattan in 1959, and that, in turn, was the speculative culmination of an endless stream of prototypes he had developed under the name 'Geodesic Domes'.

But domes are as old as the history of architecture itself. In 1784, the French architect Étienne-Louis Boullée proposed a giant dome as a monument to commemorate Sir Isaac Newton fifty years after the scientist's death. Michelangelo's dome of St Peter's Basilica dates back to 1506. The first version of the Hagia Sofia's dome, the largest interior space in the world at the time, dates back to 537 AD, and the Pantheon, the world's largest unreinforced concrete dome, to 125 AD.

Domes have been built or proposed in a myriad of materials and sizes, generally increasing with time. Where the Pantheon measured 43 metres in diameter, St Peter's dome already boasted a sphere of more than 150 metres, taller than the Great Pyramid of Giza. The largest dome seriously considered for building to date was Albert Speer's Volkshalle, the epicentre of Hitler's dreamt Germania, with a diameter of over 250 metres.

While the built manifestations have varied over time, the idea of the dome itself never changed. How could it? In its pure form, the dome owes its existence to mathematics, not architecture. The whole idea *is* its geometry. Considered as such, it is without scale and without matter.

Just as the dome is without scale and matter, it is also, perhaps inevitably, without an author. (Certainly nobody remembers the mathematician who came up with the formula.) Its use by architects does nothing to change that. The dome and any notion of an 'original work' are incompatible. It is hardly a coincidence that the architects of the two oldest examples – the Pantheon and the Hagia Sophia – remain conspicuously unknown. The dome: not exactly a typology to be precious about.

What goes for the dome goes for architecture in general: all architecture is indebted to the architecture that came before it. Yet, much like other products of human labour, architecture increasingly finds itself mired in issues of authorship – subject to copyrights, royalties, patents and other forms of IP. And not necessarily for the better.

Intellectual property is a category that includes intangible creations of the human intellect. The World Intellectual

Property Organization (WIPO) distinguishes four types of IP: patents, industrial designs, trademarks and copyright. Architecture is protected by the latter (also referred to as author's right). Copyright gives the creator (or another right holder) of an original work the exclusive right to copy, distribute, adapt, display and perform that work for a defined period of time. Works covered by copyright range from books, music, paintings, sculpture and films to computer programs, databases, advertisements, maps, technical drawings, and consequently, also building designs.[2] In the United States and the European Union, copyrights are typically protected for the duration of the life of the creator plus seventy years.

The *Oxford English Dictionary*'s earliest recording of the term 'intellectual property' is from 1769, in the *Monthly Review*, in relation to certain inventions during the first Industrial Revolution. The term was in common use by the latter half of the nineteenth century, when its meaning expanded to refer more broadly to the knowledge produced in the Industrial Revolution.

One of the first international treaties on intellectual property was the Paris Convention for the Protection of Industrial Property of 1883. Industrial property here referred to patents, trademarks, utility models, industrial designs, trade names, service marks and geographical indications as well as the 'repression of unfair competition'. It was initially signed by Belgium, Brazil, France, Guatemala, Italy, the Netherlands, Portugal, El Salvador, the Kingdom of Serbia, Spain and Switzerland. The treaty was revised and amended several times throughout the twentieth century, most recently in 1979. As of 2024, 180 countries (of 195) adhered to the convention, which makes it one of the most widely adopted treaties worldwide.

Artistic and literary copyright followed in 1886, with the Berne Convention for the Protection of Literary and Artistic Works. Instigated by Victor Hugo, the Berne Convention provided authors, musicians, poets, painters and other creators with the legal means to control how their works were used, by whom and on what terms. A treaty to the effect was signed by Belgium, France, Germany, Haiti, Italy, Liberia, Spain, Switzerland, Tunisia and the United Kingdom.

The Berne Convention was also the first ever instance in which the notion of intellectual property was tied to architecture:

> The expression 'literary and artistic works' shall include every production in the literary, scientific and artistic domain, whatever may be the mode or form of its expression, such as books, pamphlets and other writings; lectures, addresses, sermons and other works of the same nature; dramatic or dramatico-musical works; choreographic works and entertainments in dumb show; musical compositions with or without words; cinematographic works to which are assimilated works expressed by a process analogous to cinematography; works of drawing, painting, architecture, sculpture, engraving and lithography; photographic works to which are assimilated works expressed by a process analogous to photography; works of applied art; illustrations, maps, plans, sketches and three-dimensional works relative to geography, topography, architecture or science.[3]

The fact that architecture entered the equation at the Berne – and not the Paris – convention is indicative of the time: the notion of 'the original work' in architecture has its roots in

Romanticism (more about that later), which ranked buildings up there with the arts. Thus, buildings were ruled out as products to be protected as 'industrial designs', and even less as technical solutions worthy of a patent.

It wasn't until well into the next century that some very different ideas were introduced. In viewing building as a quintessentially industrial activity, the Bauhaus dispensed with the notion of buildings as one-of-a-kind artworks. Industrial production implied the prevalence of repetition over singularity, and therefore ultimately also the prevalence of the prototype over the masterpiece.

The type of architecture promoted by the Bauhaus turns questions over authorship into an anathema. What goes for the Bauhaus broadly goes for modern architecture as a whole: its prototypes, blueprints and other paradigms are meant to be repeated. They are under the unwritten obligation to acquire a life of their own irrespective of their authors. Le Corbusier's *plan libre* was literally a 'free invention', meant to be used by everyone, everywhere, all the time. His gift to humanity was the universal liberation from the constraints of the load-bearing wall. Liberation knows no author, and neither does progress. The urgencies of the twentieth century did not allow for the prohibition of reproduction under copyright. Quite the contrary: in a context of population growth, the ravages of war and the associated housing shortages, buildings pretty much evolved into a kind of generic medicine.

When it comes to architecture and the question of intellectual property, it is telling that the most high-profile authorship controversy of the twentieth century – Philip Johnson's Glass House versus Mies' Farnsworth House – never became more than a friendly dispute. The question of who copied whom never entered the legal arena. It couldn't have: the all-glass house was hardly invented by Mies either. And who do we credit for the open plan, the single span roof, the structural use of window mullions, or the lifting of a building off the ground?

The protection of intellectual property rights took a decisive turn in 1995 with the birth of the World Trade Organization (WTO), which marked the integration of IP into the global trading system. One of the driving forces was the US trade deficit, which had peaked at a record $153 billion in 1987. Blaming the more permissive IP regimes of other countries for this, the US pushed for stronger international IP protections to safeguard its IP-reliant industries: pharmaceuticals, entertainment and technology. It advocated for high standards of IP protection and robust enforcement mechanisms to ensure that member countries adopted these standards in their national laws. By linking IP protection to trade rules, the US aimed to leverage its trade relationships to ensure better compliance with IP standards by other countries. Rule-breakers would be punished and disciplined through trade provisions like tariffs and quotas.

The role of the WTO in the administering of IP has had an effect on pretty much all fields subject to copyright, covering authors, performers, sound recording producers and broadcasting organizations, geographical indications, industrial designs, integrated circuit layout designs, patents, new plant varieties, trademarks and trade names.

Although not strictly applicable to architectural designs, the change nevertheless had a profound effect on architecture too. Copyright infringement cases are steadily on the rise and increasingly happen in full view. Most prominent to date is the case of Zaha Hadid's Wangjing Soho complex: three pebble-shaped volumes up to 200 metres high, which were literally copied by a developer in Chongqing, with the two projects racing to be completed first. There was little Zaha Hadid Architects could do since 'there is no special law in China which has specific provisions on IP rights related to architecture'.[4] Chongqing Meiquan, the developer behind the Meiquan 22nd Century project, refuted accusations of copying by saying: 'Never meant to copy, only want to surpass.'[5]

The line between inspiration and plagiarism isn't always easy to draw. At the opening of Expo 2010 in Shanghai, there was a heated debate over the originality of the Chinese Pavilion. According to some, the 60-metre-high inverted pyramid was a rip-off of the Japanese Pavilion at Expo 1992 in Seville, designed by Tadao Ando; others compared it to the Canadian Pavilion at the Montreal Expo of 1967. One of the Chinese Pavilion's designers refuted the allegations by rightly pointing out that the idea of the inverted pyramid could hardly be attributed to Ando, nor was it invented in Canada.

From inverted pyramids it is a small step to the real thing. In 2008, Zahi Hawass, Secretary General of Egypt's Supreme Council of Antiquities, made a case for establishing a copyright law that would allow claims for damages against authors of reproductions of the pyramids. The new law ran into trouble before it could even be implemented. Should the Luxor Hotel in Las Vegas – the only modern pyramid-shaped building in the world according to its website – share a proportion of its profits with the Egyptian city of Luxor? That claims to this effect would leave a legal case without merit was as evident to the hotel as it was to the Egyptian secretary, who saved face by stating that despite its shape the hotel did not qualify as an exact copy since the interior differed significantly from that of the pyramids.[6] The law is yet to be adopted.

Where the Egyptian authorities failed, other proprietors of landmark buildings have succeeded. In 2003, the image of the Auditorio de Tenerife in Spain was registered as a trademark: use of it 'both in photographs and illustrations, of all or part of it as well as the use of the logo or of any other element that defines the building is regulated by the law in force on the quiet enjoyment of any registered trademark'.[7] The Auditorio charges commercial operators for using its external space for film and photography, and requires that the final product be cleared with the relevant department of the Auditorio prior to publication. A deposit is required to guarantee proper use of the images.

Beyond copyright or image rights, the design of buildings is increasingly becoming the subject of patents and trademarks too. In November 2011, Apple was granted a patent for its Upper West Side Apple Store in New York. The same design qualified for a second patent six months later. On 24 January 2013, the US Patent and Trademark Office published Apple's latest registered trademark certificate for its 'Distinctive Design & Layout' in both colour and black and white. Steve Jobs was posthumously credited as its designer. The store was the physical manifestation of his long-held creed: 'Unless we could find a way to get our message to customers at the store, we were screwed.'[8]

The significance of the Apple store patent in relation to architecture and IP can hardly be overstated. Where the original nineteenth-century definition of IP put the protection of building designs in the category of literary and artistic works, the new reality of building designs qualifying for patents and trademarks puts them in a decidedly different realm. More than 140 years after the fact, architecture has moved from the agenda of the Berne Convention to that of the Paris Convention – it is no longer a question of the arts but of an industrial design to be upheld and monetized.

While Apple was hardly the first to apply for a building design patent, it was the first to do so with consequence. In 1989, the Romanian American visual artist Radu Vero registered a patent on a multi-storied spiral building. Radu's patent, however, did not prevent Calatrava from designing the Turning Torso in Malmö in 2005. Nor did it prevent Tony Kettle from designing the Evolution Tower in Moscow in 2014, or SOM the Cayan Tower in Dubai in 2013. In 2003, OMA issued its own ironic set of patented ideas in *Content*. Needless to say, these did not prove to be effective protection against their, by now universal, copying. When it comes to enforcing IP, the legal muscle of a corporation like Apple makes all the difference.

As IP in architecture surges, so does the backlash. Initiated in 2011, Wikihouse, an open-source project for designing resource-light dwellings, has since grown to become a worldwide community of contributors. Similarly, the Open Architecture Network, formed in 2006, allows architects and engineers to share designs with a focus on sustainability under the creative commons licensing system; OpenStructures, launched in 2007, is a free database of modular projects designed on the same grid; Paperhouses, an online platform set up in 2013, allows 'world-class' architects to share housing designs for people who could never afford to hire them; Opendesk, an online platform for furniture design, also launched in 2013; OSArc (Open Source Architecture), launched the same year, promotes the use of free design software; Bricksources, an online database of parametric brickwork patterns, was formed in 2014. At the 2018 Venice Biennale, the Dutch Pavilion showed an exhibition dedicated to instigating the infringement of patents held by large corporations, using Amazon as an example.

It seems that the more precarious the condition of the market, the more the market economy tends to seek refuge in alternatives. But only as long as the precarity lasts. If the 2008 financial crisis gave rise to many of the above initiatives, it was the passing of that same crisis that sparked their dissolution. Architecture for Humanity, the charitable organization behind the Open Architecture Network, filed for bankruptcy in 2015; the Paperhouses website is no longer active. Entering the URL redirects you to the website of some anonymous real estate holding.

And then there is AI. When it comes to intellectual property, the role of AI has so far proven double-edged – at once the domain in which authorship rights are taken to their extreme, but also the field in which the absurdity of those rights is exposed. In 2019, patent applications were filed to the US, EU and UK patent offices on behalf of a machine called DABUS. Over a two-month period, DABUS had been fed words and images to 'teach' it to design a plastic food container and a flashing light. At present, the UK Patents Act of 1977 restricts inventorship to 'natural persons', as does the European Patent Convention. In the US, inventions must be the work of an 'individual'. If successful, therefore, the DABUS application will mark a decisive change: it will be the first time a machine has been recognized as a creator by patent offices.

According to DABUS's initiator, the ultimate purpose of the patent application was to get some clarity concerning the laws and rules covering AI-generated inventions: to help ensure that people and machines are appropriately credited for their work. '[We should] incentivize innovation by rewarding inventive activity, regardless of its source, [and] insure we acknowledge people for their inventive work, without taking credit for the work of others, and for acknowledging the accomplishments of AI developers.'[9] The response of the European Patent Office (EPO) was as conclusive as it was brief: its present legal position does not allow AI systems to be considered as inventors, and no change in this position should be expected in the near future.

DABUS stands for 'Device for the Autonomous Bootstrapping of Unified Sentience'. Unwittingly (or perhaps not), the name reveals how its accomplishments are built on the work of myriad others. The raw material on which DABUS draws is, in principle, everything on the internet. The case shows how, in the context of AI, the notion of authorship is blurred by definition: everything created by someone is cocreated with everyone else. The only honest answer to the question 'who is the author?' is simply: 'everyone!' Any other answer, even the attribution to an anonymous machine, will be nothing but a form of legalized theft.

The arts were the last bastion in which the notion of authorship could be credibly entertained. (In ordinary work, the idea has long suffered a quiet death.) But the arts too, are changing, with cocreation, hybrid authorships, contested copyrights and, as outlined above, the permanent ambiguity between human and machine as a result of AI. The Romantic notion underpinning the Berne Convention hardly applies any longer. The fate of originality and authorship is akin to that of the work of art in the age of mechanical reproduction. They may continue to be upheld, but they can never be the same again. No longer are they absolute, or even relevant.

Still, one wonders: is it really AI that drives this profound change, or does AI simply make visible something that has long been the case? The latter seems especially true in the domain of architecture. What applies to AI equally applies to architecture. Every work of architecture incorporates the work of the many architects who came before. Who invented the floor, the ceiling, the roof (pitched or flat), the door, the wall, the stair, the window, the balcony, the corridor, the escalator, the elevator? Would architecture even exist if the use of these were prohibited by law? The preoccupation with authorship only breeds impossible questions.

Patents in medicine are often the result of research and development that can cost billions. Yet the average patent in medicine lasts no more than twenty years. 'Research' by architects, in contrast, mainly involves studying the work of others; yet IP rights on buildings last for seventy years after the death of their author. According to this law, we will be entitled to use the designs of Frank Lloyd Wright in 2029, those of Le Corbusier in 2035, and those of Oscar Niemeyer in 2082. The works of architects emulated ad nauseam can be freely copied when the world no longer has a use for them.

Comparing architecture to the visual arts or music is a gross misrepresentation. Unlike the latter, architecture has a public duty. To fulfil that duty, it is not only unavoidable but imperative that its ideas are copied – and altered, bastardized, corrupted, mutilated, until they ultimately disappear into new ideas. Originality is one of architecture's most enduring myths. Copyrights, royalties, patents and other forms of protectionist IP have no place in architecture. Its ideas are meant to be stolen. Evolution in architecture doesn't exist without counterfeit copies. Even the ideas we desperately try to protect through copyright inevitably owe their existence to other ideas. There is nothing original about buildings.

Who owns ideas? Those who have them? The assumption is that IP protection stimulates innovation, which in turn helps the economy. But there is no conclusive evidence of a correlation between IP rights protection and economic growth. It seems that corporations, not national economies, are the strongest beneficiaries. Nowhere is this more manifest than in the pharmaceutical industry, dominated as it is by a few large medical corporations, commonly referred to as Big Pharma, for whom IP has become the major source of revenue. The dominant position of the big corporations is the source of increasing worry and protest, being representative of an undesirable trend in which intellectual property is increasingly a euphemism for intellectual monopoly.

As more and more fields move to protect their inventions to ensure financial security, please let architecture be the outspoken exception. The fight against climate change is going to require all we can muster. Sovereign fences will have to be broken down in favour of a wholesale mobilization. In that context, the insistence on intellectual property or authorship rights is highly inappropriate, and any architecture staking its claims on them a doomed business – no more moral than the tobacco industry.

It is a given that most of the built environment is not built by starchitects. In fact, most of it materializes without architects ever being involved. The notion of the 'original genius' – a unique human being with visionary powers – was a myth constructed by the German Romantics over two centuries ago. The concept has come to haunt the arts as much as it does architecture. In its name, architecture must side with the masterpiece against the cliché, with the unique against the common, with the specific against the generic, with the exception over the rule and with the margins over the mainstream. We aspire to be the first, not the best. After the first, there is nothing. (Which conveniently ensures that the first is also the best.) The ingrained obligation to produce 'original works' forces architects to continuously operate against the odds. Not only are there too few (original) ideas to cover the combined total of projects underway globally, but the insistence on originality also bars architecture from using the body of its own ideas. In denying ourselves access to our collective memory, we deny ourselves a common future. Progress is the original work's first casualty.

A hundred and forty years after the Berne Convention, let's abolish authorship! We are nearing the end of the play. Imminent is the downfall of characters who have built their success on owning the ideas of others and failing to take responsibility for it. Let the final act be their *demasqué.* Not the great architects, but their definitive impossibility.

The Dome was never built. Neither were any of the designs proposed by the other starchitects. I ran into the Japanese architect the other day. We reminisced about our time in Russia. She spoke English perfectly.

6

After Taste

'How is this Jeddah?'

We are caught off guard. Not a question we had seen coming. As far as we're concerned, our design proposal is Jeddah all the way. The project mimics the logic of the city hosting it. Its plan is a scaled-down version of a piece of Jeddah's urban fabric. A maze-like structure of meandering walls frames a diverse series of internal and outside spaces. A series of interconnected courtyards – *barajas* in local terms – allows the public to pass through the building without having to enter any of its interior spaces, which, in turn, can be divided among individual tenants. We should be golden.

The project is both a developer's dream and a perfect tribute to the climate in which it must sit. All outside spaces are comfortably protected from the wind, the dust and, most importantly, the all-consuming heat. Our engineers have calculated that, even with summer temperatures reaching up to 50 degrees Celsius, temperatures in the exterior spaces will never be more than 25 degrees. Even the project's method of construction – rammed earth – draws from a local inspiration. In short, we fail to see the point of the question. How is this *not* Jeddah? Given the nature of what we have proposed, the answer seems self-evident.

But clearly not for our client. He proceeds to ask another question: 'How about the DNA of the place?' The question acquires the status of an instruction: 'What we really want to see is not design, not architecture, but really the DNA of the place!'

Silence ensues.

'Jedda'ah!', he repeats, adding an extra syllable in exasperation.

We are no clearer. Another silence ensues.

Where do we go from here? Our client clearly feels misunderstood, but equally so do we.

Would we like another coffee?

We're fine. (We obviously aren't.)

We are at an impasse. What *is* 'the DNA of the place'? What is he getting at, this newly appointed CEO of the so-called 'special purpose vehicle' acting as our client body? We know he has been flown in from Egypt and is no more Jeddawi than we are. Still, how do we respond? We are keen to bounce back, come up with a diplomatic way to convey that our ideas, even if not literally, all owe deeply to the place that is Jedda'ah.

We never even make it to the first sentence. Our internal deliberations are cut short by the CEO gesticulating to one of his assistants, who promptly hands him a big stack of foam boards.

One by one, the CEO begins to turn the boards, which must have been prepared well in advance of our arrival.

'You see . . . It's all about the details', he explains. The boards hold various photographs and material samples. These 'mood boards', we are told, will give us an indication of the desired look and feel of the project. The photographs, all taken from the CEO's Instagram account, are of various interiors like the ones they have in mind. The material samples are the suggested finishes (or similar). Each new board is different from the previous, causing the number of references and possible finishes to multiply at a dazzling pace. Our emphatically minimalist design proposal becomes more baroque with each image or sample he suggests we incorporate.

We wonder: are we looking at a proposed evolution of our project, or at a proposed alternative? But what alternative exactly? The CEO's vision for the project can only be summed up as 'more specifically everything'. Contrary to what has been suggested, there is no unique Jeddah DNA waiting to be discovered, just a universe of infinite possibilities between which it is impossible to choose.

Someone in the room presses a key on a laptop. Music fills the space. 'Did you know that we already have a tune for the project?' We are startled. A faint smile runs across the CEO's otherwise stern face, deeply moved by what sounds like a fusion mix of Anouar Brahem and Burt Bacharach. For the first time that afternoon, he looks genuinely content. He is happy, and our less-than-satisfactory performance does nothing to diminish that.

We're at a loss as to how to proceed.

We've all been there. That inevitable point in the process when the logical progression of decisions breaks down. The moment 'taste' enters the equation. What colour should the walls be? What material should be selected for the kitchen worktops? What finishes should there be on the floors of the sanitary facilities? What atmosphere should be created? What ought to be the theme of each space?

No longer can things be argued; they must be felt. They're up for grabs, to be decided by whoever in the room feels most strongly. The fun has started, and it's no fun. Extensive client sessions are supposed to facilitate the decisions, but they only highlight further the arbitrary nature of pending choices – each option interchangeable with the next. Character only exists in the plural, and therefore not at all. It is impossible to take decisions. There is no clarity, other than on the futility of the subjects under consideration.

Rational, yet frivolous; logical, yet obscure . . . Architecture is and remains a hopeless hybrid: neither art nor science, craft nor trade. Once the most important decisions have been made, the work invariably disintegrates into a fruitless soul-searching, a pointless pursuit of 'a certain *je ne sais quoi*'. The architect becomes a carpetbagger expected to give physical shape to the vaguest qualifications: warm, soft, tasty, timeless, chic, feminine, conversational, balanced, layered, robust, urban, Japanese . . . Adjectives take the place of arguments, until finally the adjectives too run out and only a meditative stare at the mood board is left. All the while, we pretend we understand. All the while, we don't. We are like the prisoners in Plato's cave: perceiving only shadows.

Could technology save us? Could computational intelligence liberate us from the hopelessly arbitrary nature of what we deem architectural design?

The above scene took place in the summer of 2022. In November of that year, OpenAI's GPT-3.5, better known as ChatGPT, was launched – the world's first commercially available artificial intelligence program. Others followed. In February 2023, both Meta and Microsoft released their own language models to compete with ChatGPT: Llama and Copilot. GPT-4 was launched in March 2023. In July, Anthropic, a company founded by several former OpenAI employees, released Claude 2. Its successor, Claude 3, was introduced in March 2024. In December that year, Google launched its own competitor to ChatGPT – Gemini. The AI boom was a fact.

If at the time these events seemed much ado about nothing when it came to architecture, that quickly changed as the full potential of these programs became clear. From text analysis it was a small step to image analysis. GPT-4 was able to process both text and image inputs. Where Claude 2 was able to read PDFs and other documents, Claude 3 was also able to analyze images. Google's Gemini, too, was capable of working with both text and image.

The ability to generate visuals was taken to extremes by the public availability as of 2022 of programs such as DALL-E 2 (OpenAI) and Midjourney beta (Midjourney, Inc.), both able to generate complex images from simple text prompts. In August 2022, British startup Stability AI had released Stable Diffusion, for which, unlike DALL-E and Midjourney, the code and model weights were made public. Since March 2023, Adobe Cloud subscribers have had Firefly integrated in Adobe programs. In December 2023, Google launched its Imagen 2.

And it didn't stop there. In November 2023, Runway, a New York City-based startup funded by Google, Nvidia and Salesforce Ventures, opened the door to text-video generative models with its Gen-2. Gen-3 Alpha was launched in June 2024, marking a step towards building what they call general world models, described on their website as 'an AI system that builds an internal representation of an environment, and uses it to simulate future events within that environment'.[1]

Musicians were not exempt: AIVA (2016) helps craft classical compositions; Endel (2018) creates soundscapes to match user activities (relaxation, focus, sleep, moving and so on); while Google's Lyria and Meta's AudioCraft (both 2023) generate all types of music from text prompts.

The work of architects too, is profoundly affected – and not just in terms of image production. In addition to visualization programs such as DALL-E and Midjourney, apps like Autodesk Forma (formerly Spacemaker, acquired by Autodesk in 2020) help architects (and clients) generate site proposals by combining data on building regulations, climate conditions and solar exposure.

Alternatives to Forma include TestFit (2017), aimed at developers, architects and contractors who want to 'maximize site potential and get the right deals done faster',[2] and Archistar (2018), which enables the user to 'find and reveal the highest & best use of any site'.[3] There are also several plan generating apps: Maket, PlanFinder, Qbiq, OPAL and Planner 5D Floor Plan Creator, to name but a few. More than for architects, these apps allow novices to create 'accurate' floor plans with ease.

Architecture may be a small thing to the world of AI, but AI is a big thing to the world of architecture. The number of architects estimated to soon lose their jobs to AI varies from zero to 90 per cent. Despite (or perhaps because of) the predicted job losses, there is a serious curiosity among architects about AI – a level of engagement that we haven't seen for quite some time, myself included. As I'm writing this, two years have passed since our client meeting in Jeddah. I can't help but wonder what might have been different had we gone through that experience with the aid of the new technology.

I decide to conduct a little experiment. I open the browser on my laptop and go to dall-efree.com. I type: 'Do me a building that is Jeddah.' I have decided to put the machine through the exact same treatment that we were subjected to. The first result is predictable: a small, six-story building with Roshan windows, covered in Hejazi patterns and surrounded by palm trees – the stuff of postcards, a feel which is further enhanced by using a sepia filter. We know that, with OpenAI, the sources cannot be revealed, but the image has the British military archives written all over it – clearly not a building we would ever do.

I refine my search and type: 'Do me an OMA building that is Jeddah.' What appears is a tall steel structure, part Vierendeels, part cross-braced, with three hovering volumes under what appears to be a thundering sky. Twelve-lane roads surround the building on all sides. In the background we see the skyline of a city, which we must assume is Jeddah. Still, the tallest and most recognizable icon featured is Kingdom Tower, which is not actually in Jeddah, but in Riyadh. When it comes to depicting foreign lands, OpenAI is about as accurate as Hollywood.

Just for the hell of it, I do the same search again, this time adding the extra syllable: 'Do me an OMA building that is Jedda'ah.' The alternative spelling has no bearing on the search result. The same image appears, albeit with slightly more intense cross-bracing. (Kingdom Tower remains ever present.)

I decide to add the exclamation mark, hoping to capture at least some of the client's exasperation: 'Do me an OMA building that is Jedda'ah!' This time, a very different image appears: a series of stacked boxes forming a vertical ring around a central void. The whole thing is reminiscent of the aquarium we designed for Hamburg's HafenCity. It is striking how, even eighty years after the fact, the exclamation mark remains the perfect encapsulation of the German spirit. Rip-offs and stereotypes – they seem to live their finest hour in the universe of AI.

The height is a problem. The building we proposed in the real world was low-rise, only two stories high. AI is meant to get closer to the situation we experience in practice. Not a difficult one to correct, one would assume. I type: 'Do me a two-story OMA building that is Jedda'ah!' The image I get complies with the instruction I've given. At least, it does technically. The building is indeed two, occasionally three, stories high. (Again, Kingdom Tower features in the background, its distinct shape modified to resemble an hourglass. Evidently the prompts entered affect the context too.) But there is something funny about the building that emerges. Yes, it is (mostly) two stories high, but the height of those two stories in no way conforms to the customary floor height of buildings – in Jeddah or anywhere else for that matter. The floors are much, much taller. And thus even a building emphatically intended to be a low-rise structure becomes a mini skyscraper. The whole idea of OMA doing a modest building is not believable apparently, at least not in the world of OpenAI.

I decide to move on to the building's interior. After all, the interior was the focus of our client's comments, and the part of the project most difficult for us to get a handle on. I type: 'Show me the interior of a two-story OMA building in Jedda'ah!' I'm given a view of a small building, but still from the outside. (It seems the idea of OMA designing interiors is no more believable than the idea of it designing low-rise buildings.) Through the large opening in the facade, I get a hint of the interior space – an Eames-like lightness of steel and concrete panelling, ornated with sparse modern furniture (not ours). The contrast with the exterior, a timber frame filled in with mud, could not be greater. The interior has absolutely nothing to do with the building it is in. Again, not a design philosophy we would easily embrace – at least not here, not now, and not like this.

Interiors are best viewed on their own, without the exterior interfering with one's judgement. I decide to go all out. I type: 'Show me the interior of a two-story OMA building in Jedda'ah, that is also warm, soft, tasty, timeless, chic, feminine, conversational, balanced, layered, robust, urban and Japanese!' The machine seems to be thinking about my prompt for a very long time . . . Just as I'm about to give up, an image pops up. Unexpectedly, the result is strangely convincing. It is the type of interior I know from hotels, the kind that caters to a clientele with a penchant for a somewhat subtle opulence. I guess this is what they call 'prompt crafting'.

'Denmark with a touch of the Middle East' is perhaps the best way to sum up the image on screen in words. Although the inverse – the Middle East with a touch of Denmark –

would apply just as well. The accidental similarity between the colour of the desert and that of Scandinavian furniture offers boundless perspectives. Sand and timber. It is exactly the type of image we know everyone wants but are consistently unable to produce: originality as the sum of all clichés.

I ponder for a moment, reflecting on the experiment I have just conducted. Underneath some of the images there is text: fragments of sentences, scrambled together from miscellaneous sources, amalgamated into slogans supposedly to support each image. Not a single one makes sense. On closer inspection, neither do any of the images. Traditional building methods carry implausibly futuristic details; radical chic supports understated luxury, and the forces of gravity are at once honoured and defied. Style conventions, architectural syntax, laws of construction, building economy and other analogue absolutes fade into perfect insignificance in a universe of perpetual digital entropy.

Looking at images created by others, it is impossible to reconstruct which prompts have gone into which image. Each reference is as familiar as it is untraceable. There are no choices; there is only accumulation. Unlikely encounters too: Frank Lloyd Wright meets UN Studio; Erich Mendelsohn meets Stefano Boeri; Frank Gehry meets Friedensreich Hundertwasser; Robert Venturi meets Massimiliano Fuksas. AI = Imre Makovecz reborn; AI = Freddy Mamani minus Bolivia; AI = Berdimuhamedov's dream. Obedience and disobedience meet in perfect sync. A sacred rule is broken with every new option generated. Magically, the result is a curious apotheosis of compliance: all boxes ticked.

I am as excited as I am unsettled.

Let's theorize for a moment. How does AI actually work? Just as statistics enable infinite permutations from limited numbers, AI enables infinite combinations from existing, and therefore finite, references. The internet represents the largest repository of things ever created by humankind. In its current form, it treads a fine line between the countless and the infinite. AI is what definitively makes it cross that line. If, before AI, the internet was a means to collect and collate, after AI it becomes a means to create.

No longer do we have to add to what exists by inventing new things. From here on, invention is automated, a matter of combining, recombining, reconfiguring and recycling everything that has existed up to this moment. As our past inventions take on a mutant life of their own, we become spectators in the context of our own creations, which proliferate around us like vegetation. Human artefacts assume a second lease of life as nature. *Homo sapiens* is a primitive settler once again.

'The situations into which the product of mechanical reproduction can be brought may not touch the actual work of art, yet the quality of its presence is always depreciated.'[4] Walter Benjamin's *The Work of Art in the Age of Mechanical Reproduction* was published nearly 100 years ago. His observations hardly spelled the end of art though. The processes of mechanical reproduction in question – photography and film – have long earned their rightful place among the arts. It is safe to assume that over time AI creations will do the same. Tim Fu (ex-Zaha Hadid Architects), an emerging star in the world of architecture and AI, signs his creations as though they are authentically his own – not drawn, but 'prompted'.

As art evolves, so do art forms. After Pop Art comes Prompt Art. Benjamin's last project, 'The Project of Quotes', can be read as a precursor. In a final phase, the articulation of his own thought was best served by a composite of the words of others. The originality of the method takes primacy over the unoriginality of the substance it uses. What film and photography were to art, the book of quotes was (meant to be) to writing. The project was never finished. A century on, AI urges another book. The work of art in the age of automated creation. Or, more plainly, 'creative work in the age of automated creation'.

If the Industrial Revolution brought about machines that escalated to an extreme the output of physical labour, AI brings about a similar escalation in terms of thought labour. We no longer need to spend time conceiving; we command. Result bears no relation to effort. A few words suffice to generate the most sophisticated products. If they are not to one's liking, synonyms will generate different results in an instant. The most elaborate building designs emerge at the touch of a fingertip. No longer do the confines of the possible represent a plausible limit on our limitless desires. 'What you see is what you get' is an outmoded cliché that reflects an outmoded ethos. With AI, you can get whatever you get to see. Design choices don't have to be any more heavy-handed than a shopping spree. Legitimately so. Faster, and less ambiguous.

Buildings are still confined by building technology, and reductionist aesthetics are still synonymous with expediency. But not for much longer. What AI is to the process of conception, 3D printing will be to the process of building itself. Together they will dismantle the last great bastion of physical labour: the construction industry. The machine age nears its completion as automation rules. No more foremen, construction workers or supervisors. Workers' villages and portacabins will be a thing of the past as the act of building becomes instantaneous. Press 'B' for building. Architects can sit back and relax while contractors can go home. Unexpected collateral ensues – including the revival of tropical tax havens, fuelled by billions stocked up in pension funds waiting to be released.

'Form follows function', 'form follows fiction', 'form follows fiasco', 'form follows folly' . . . In the end, most likely, form will simply follow form, stripped of values and morality. Unwittingly, the new technology brings back an old notion: that of style. Ornament, a sin in the context of modern architecture's original mission – a wilful waste of time and resources – becomes an express possibility again. No longer is ornament dependent on a life devoted to craft; it can be invoked, perfected or discarded at will. In the age of AI, Adolf Loos's *Ornament and Crime* gets its long-awaited sequel, simply titled *Ornament!*

The success of the sequel will be short-lived, however. The easier an ornament is to generate, the more ornate it tends to get. Symbols and signs intensify until all comprehension of them breaks down, even the comprehension of them as mere symbols and signs. In a recent series of AI-generated interiors, an excess of digitally generated ornament creates the impression of cobwebs – not the result of careful decoration and upkeep, but of a lack of maintenance. Excess is AI's middle name: ornament is exaggerated to the point of waste, the organic to the point of the macabre, green to the point of putrid, until only a funeral procession of interchangeable images is left. In its ultimate form, AI marks a triumph not of the will but of the whim. The abstract white room – one day it might appear wonderfully exotic again.

The prospects for interactivity are boundless. Just as the iPhone turns everyone into a photographer, AI turns everyone into an architect. Prompt crafting requires no architectural education or background. All it requires are words. Anyone with basic literacy can participate. The art of architecture becomes like the art of conversation. The views of clients, users, stakeholders, or whoever else might wish to be involved, can be welcomed, tested and incorporated on the spot. Snobbish dismissal of lay opinions is a thing of the past. The most elitist profession can adopt the most egalitarian ways. Finally.

All pretences notwithstanding, the democratization of architecture fostered through AI proves double-edged. Yes, it spells the end of the authority of architects as we know it – every non-architect is as good as every architect – yet at the same time it propels some to ever greater levels of fame. Particularly for architects who are no longer with us. In the context of AI, immortality has become a real and lasting prospect. After musicians and movie stars, it is architects who get to live forever, adding new works to their oeuvre well after their passing. Le Corbusier never really left us after all, and Zaha Hadid gets to live on in Patrik Schumacher – forever. The architect is dead; long live the architect.

Shenzhen Bay International Hotel, 2023. Anonymous boxes in an anonymous setting. Much is being said about the blessings of AI: a technology fostering a smoother, more streamlined process from inception to construction, producing instant cost calculations, automated construction packages and guaranteed compliant specifications. Still, if the world's first fully AI-generated building is anything to go by, architecture after AI feels a lot like architecture before AI – the promised gains as hyped as they are indiscernible.

We've been there before: new technologies promising new revolutions. In the 1980s, the introduction of AutoCAD was expected to make entire armies of draughtsmen redundant and drastically reduce working hours for the few that remained. Today, architects work longer hours than ever. New technologies did nothing to change that; they merely raised expectations. We save time only to spend more time.

Time and again the duplicitous nature of the concept of efficiency reveals itself. The more efficient we become, the more we are enslaved by the ever-accelerating rut of things. The age of the machine gave birth to Taylorist work processes aimed at increasing productivity and reducing costs. Today, Taylorism is synonymous with the ruthless extraction of human labour. A similar writing is on the wall with AI: cultural workers supervising an increasingly automated process, producing interchangeable content around the clock, their performance measured against the efficiency (or any synonym thereof) of the plans and layouts churned out by machines.

Is there an alternative? What if we approach things from the other direction? What if the real potential of AI resides not in expediency or efficiency, but in the opposite – in cultivating our inefficiency and irrationality? Might we view AI not as a form of superior intelligence, but as a welcome opportunity to delegate erroneous human behaviour to the machine? AI: the outsourcing not of mundane but of frivolous tasks. Imagine the benefits. No longer do we have to fret over choices of material, interior design, themes, 'brand identity' or other peripheral concerns. We can delegate the tiresome burden of artificially imposing a character on buildings that already have one. The machine caters to whatever request, no matter how whimsical or random. Our perceived arrogance will be a thing of the past: with help of AI, we enter into conversation, listen, optioneer, only to stop when time runs out; we can reengage with our patrons, our users, the public and so on.

Architecture is hardly the only field grappling with the implications of AI. Having been beaten by IBM's Deep Blue in 1997, the then world chess champion Garry Kasparov came up with the concept of 'Centaur Chess'. Rather than viewing artificial intelligence as a replacement for human intelligence, he proposed that human players work alongside AI chess engines to form a 'Centaur' team. While AI provided the computational analysis and pattern recognition, the human players retained their primacy in terms of strategic thinking. This hybrid approach outperformed both AI and human players on their own; witness the victories of AI-assisted amateur players over grandmasters as well as over the most advanced AI engines of the time.

Blind trust or unfettered skepsis? The idea of Centaur Chess represents a more nuanced way of thinking about the role of AI – a shift from the prevailing view that it is simply taking over human tasks to viewing it as a partner in human work. The concept extends beyond chess. Already, fields like medicine, design and business benefit from AI generating, filtering and testing ideas at a speed no human can match. In none of these fields does AI render human expertise obsolete; when used wisely – not to think for us but to help us think more clearly – it enhances that expertise.

While the results of my first ever DALL-E experiment may have been comical, AI already presents a clear and present opportunity to revolutionize the architectural process – a much-needed chance to rid architecture of certain persistent dilemmas; a means to unwind the unfortunate entanglement of logic and taste, of objectivity and subjectivity; a way to rise above frivolous choices, not by not making them, but by delegating them so we can focus on the important things. Rely on AI for matters of taste. Humankind's ultimate liberation will be the delegation of fun.

The Jeddah project was never finished. Our client body got swallowed by one of the country's big developers. The Egyptian CEO was 'called to other duties' (read: fired) in the middle of further negotiations. We were never formally notified of his departure. It is rumoured that his tasks were taken over by AI.

We are still awaiting payment.

7

Flourish in the Field

'We understand that you're a real architect? Brick and mortar – that sort of thing?'

Cambridge University, early October 2019: Leaving Ceremony for the Sir Arthur Marshall Visiting Professor of Urban Design. The end of his term is the beginning of mine.

The question feels very uncomfortable. My predecessor clearly didn't know about brick and mortar. Why would he? He is a filmmaker. He studied architecture once, but if he ever practised it those days are long gone. It is not even certain that the outgoing professor holds an architecture degree. His bio is inconclusive in this regard. His credentials are those of an eminent filmmaker, writer, artist and exhibition curator – with numerous research positions, exhibitions, publications and books to his name.

The results of his one-year term are mysterious, to say the least. His closing address, delivered in the college's intimate, all-timber lecture theatre, doesn't make things much clearer. Students have been asked to 'study' a former limestone quarry in north Oxford, primarily by crossing it on foot, for days, sometimes weeks, taking in the atmosphere, breathing the air, tasting the soil . . . all so that they can become one with the place and imagine its future.

Or not. Leaving the site 'as is' also qualifies as an outcome, we hear. And that is exactly what most students seem to have done. We get to see slides of the work, mostly a photographic record of their hikes as well as the occasional short film, each of which seems to last a lifetime. (The filmmaker is a known Tarkovsky admirer.) Outside the lecture hall, there is a detailed model of the quarry in its present state. The only real object of 'design' is the model's base: a thin, rusty steel frame. That, and the retro-futuristic sound installation next to it, playing music that seems to come directly off a yoga playlist.

The outgoing professor is thanked extensively for his efforts over drinks. One of the endowed professorships' sponsors comes up to him to convey how much he enjoyed the presentation. He confesses to knowing the words but not quite the meaning they acquired in the sentences. Without awaiting the ex-professor's reaction, the sponsor moves on to inquire about the next professor's knowledge of brick and mortar. I feel decidedly put on the spot.

We go for dinner afterwards, in Jesus College's Great Dining Hall. Its long tables evoke scenes from Harry Potter. As does the hall itself: Hogwarts School of Witchcraft and Wizardry at the mercy of contemporary lighting consultants. Masters of bygone times look on from the walls – the custodians of a tradition going back all the way to 1496. I wonder about the type of extracurricular activities these men might have engaged in. Just as I'm trying to estimate the combined length of avoided prison time, I hear my name being called: 'Can the incoming professor please stand up and say a few words?'

I have a confession to make. I may be a licensed architect, but I have zero idea of brick and mortar. The obligation to spend at least one semester on a construction site was abolished the year before I entered university, and I've never liked them since. When it comes to the waning status of construction work within architecture education, I'm a specimen of the trend. Guilty as charged!

I held the position at Cambridge for three years, and in none of them was there even the remotest focus on building. The first year was spent studying the economy of architecture – in part allowing me to write this book; the second was spent preparing for and collating the results of a field trip to Africa – we did to Africa what my predecessor did to the Oxford quarry: 'leave as is'; and the third and last year was dedicated to a theme titled 'The Benefits of Megalomania' – the perfect way to avoid attention to detail, construction detail included.

Architecture schools are typically accused of being divorced from reality. In that sense, critical comments about the lack of 'brick and mortar' in the professional training of architects are nothing new. Witnessing the multitude of recent 'building' initiatives at architecture schools, one could even argue that such criticism has not fallen on deaf ears.

At the Bartlett, students build temporary pavilions in the Queen Elizabeth Olympic Park in East London each spring, to 'test engineering and architectural ideas to their limits'.[1] In the department of Advanced Design Studies at the

University of Tokyo, students build a pavilion each year to 'research new ways of collaboration between humans and machines'.[2] In 2011, architecture students at the University of Stuttgart built the ICD/ITKE Research Pavilion, described as a 'temporary, bionic research pavilion made of wood at the intersection of teaching and research'.[3] In 2016, thirty-two students from ETH Zurich conceived and built the Pavilion of Reflections for Manifesta 11, the nomadic, European biennial of contemporary art, which was hosted by Zurich that year. The pavilion was a floating wooden structure on Lake Zurich used for cinema screenings and as a public swimming pool. In 2019, around 150 first-year students at EPFL, in Lausanne, Switzerland, produced a series of wooden structures that were meant to revive the area around La Buvette d'Evian – a modernist building on the French shore of Lake Geneva, designed by Jean Prouvé in the 1950s. The students' projects, which included a projection screen, a garden, a lookout area, a greenhouse, water swings and a bird wall, were inaugurated at an event organized by the city of Evian. In 2021, TU Delft organized a student competition to build a 'sustainable, circular and modular' pavilion for 'exhibitions and presentations on innovations concerning nature, health and a sustainable future' at the Soestdijk Palace, the former residence of Queen Juliana of the Netherlands.[4]

Some universities go further and offer entire courses on design and building. Ever since 1967, the Jim Vlock First Year Building Project at the Yale School of Architecture has given students the chance to design and build a structure as part of their graduate education. Among the earliest projects realized through the programme were a series of community centres in Appalachia and camp buildings in Connecticut. More recently, partnerships with various NGOs have resulted in affordable housing projects. Since 1993, Rural Studio, an off-campus design-build programme at the School of Architecture of Auburn University, has given students a 'more hands-on educational experience while assisting an under-served population in West Alabama's Black Belt region'.[5] At the University of Kansas, the Studio 804 course tasks students to develop a residence or university building from 'preliminary mock-ups to laying the foundation to the landscaping – all over a nine-month period'.[6] The course has existed since 1995. The DesignBuildUTAH programme at the University of Utah's School of Architecture offers students the opportunity to 'build a full-scale work of architecture in collaboration with the Navajo Nation in southeastern Utah'.[7] The programme was founded by journalist-turned-architect Hank Louis in 2004.

And then there is the revival of architecture schools entirely dedicated to practice, such as the one initially established at Taliesin by Frank Lloyd Wright and his wife Olgivanna, born out of their belief that students should learn by doing. In 1986, the programme was registered as an architecture school and today it continues Wright's legacy as The School of Architecture (TSOA). After a brief spell at Paolo Soleri's Cosanti and Arcosanti, the school relocated to Cattle Track Arts in Scottsdale, Arizona. Its website reassures us that 'the students continue to learn experientially, augmented by more formal classes and workshops'.[8]

Brick and mortar. How literally should the words be taken? Are they a plea to make construction knowledge the core of architectural education again, as in the above programmes? Or do the implications run deeper, indicative of a larger discomfort with the state of architecture education in general – estranged from the apparent priorities of the world at large? Does 'brick and mortar' really mean 'brick and mortar', or does it mean something much broader: the desire to reengage with the practicalities of the physical – that is *real* – world (and not just that of the Cambridge sponsor)?

Views on the intimate, and necessary, relation between the theory and practice of building appear to be remarkably consistent throughout history. The English translations of the titles of their most important works – *Ten Books on Architecture* and *Ten Books of Architecture* – put Vitruvius and Alberti perfectly on the same page. One the incarnation of the other. It is through a distinction in tone, however, that key differences become manifest:

> Architects who have aimed at acquiring manual skill without scholarship have never been able to reach a position of authority to correspond to their pains, while those who relied only upon theories and scholarship were obviously hunting the shadow, not the substance. But those who have a thorough knowledge of both, like men armed at all points, have the sooner attained their object and carried authority with them.
>
> Vitruvius, *De architectura*[9]

> Him I call an Architect, who, by sure and wonderful Art and Method, is able, both with Thought and Invention, to devise, and, with Execution, to complete all those Works, which, by means of the Movement of great Weights, and the Conjunction and Amassment of Bodies, can, with the greatest Beauty, be adapted to the Uses of Mankind: And

> to be able to do this, he must have a thorough Insight into the noblest and most curious Sciences. Such must be the Architect.
>
> Leon Battista Alberti, *De re aedificatoria*[10]

Where Vitruvius' *De architectura* presumes a reciprocal relationship – no theory without practice, no practice without theory – the reified description of the architect in Alberti's *De re aedificatoria* makes no secret of the hierarchical relationship implied. In any relation there is an inferior party, and for Alberti that is clearly not the architect. Alberti originally studied law at the University of Bologna. A preoccupation with law also transpires in his writing about building. What is an observation with Vitruvius acquires the status of an edict with Alberti – no practice without theory!

Alberti's theories saw the architect elevated to the status of the judge – a figure, like the pope or the king, able to confer his divine judgement. Alberti's conception of the architect as judge forever changed the relation between theory and practice. Not only does it mark the first formal separation between the two, it also makes such a separation desirable, even mandatory. Judgement – the act of deciding – can only ever be effectuated in full if it remains fully separated from execution.

Ironically, the empowerment of the architect as judge, removed from execution, de facto coincided with a conceding of power. Observing a strict separation between judgement and execution prohibits the latter from informing the former. Without a real knowledge of practice, architects can only survive by resorting to other means of asserting their authority – an authority that they no longer have per se.

Alberti's view of architecture condemned the architect to turn to rhetoric, especially to the use of visual representation as a rhetorical tool. The elaborate use of illustrations in the architectural treatises of the Renaissance can be seen in this light. More than ever, architecture came to rely on drawing, both as a way for the architect to convey his intentions to the client and a way to hold the workers executing those intentions accountable. The drawing represented the perfect language to both patron and craftsman. (In passing, it also conveniently made sure the two never spoke.)

The language of drawing would change the professional life of the architect forever, as a means par excellence to exercise authority, taught and promoted by the academic institutions established in Italy and later France. (In both languages, drawing and designing translate into the same word: *disegno* and *desinner.*)

In 1563, Giorgio Vasari established the Accademia e Compagnia delle Arti del Disegno (later renamed Accademia del Disegno) in Florence under the patronage of Cosimo de Medici. The academy taught painting, sculpture and architecture as the three arts of drawing. Similar institutions were founded in Perugia (1573), Rome (1577) and Milan (1610).

In 1648, the Académie royale de peinture et de sculpture was established in Paris. Cities across Europe followed the model. After the French Revolution, the Académie was reorganized as the renamed Académie des Beaux-Arts. More academies of its kind were established across Europe and the Americas.

The Beaux Arts tradition continued where Alberti had left off. With great success, one could argue. The intellectual separation between theory and practice, between thinking and doing, design and execution, drawing and building, has remained the norm within architecture education to date. 'The manual Operator being no more than an Instrument to the Architect.'[11]

An interesting experiment in bridging the divide occurred at the German Bauhaus in the first half of the twentieth century. Even though its first director, Walter Gropius, insisted that the goal of Bauhaus was building, the school was not created with a proper architecture department. Real-life projects were undertaken only as part of his office, where students could do what we would call an internship today. In 1926, in response to the students' discontent, Gropius agreed to establish an architecture department and asked Hannes Meyer to be its head. Meyer was a known proponent of the idea that the architect was a worker like any other. When he succeeded Gropius as director two years later, he expanded the Bauhaus's staff and diversified its curriculum with classes in technical installations, heat insulation, standardization, building construction and the organization and financing of the construction process.

Under Meyer, the school took on projects like the 'experimental houses' for the municipality of Dessau, a house for a dentist, a school in Bernau, the redevelopment of the municipal library and the remodelling of the transport office, both also in Dessau, and a retirement home in Frankfurt am Main. Students were involved by means of a contract with the school's building department. Their tasks varied from obtaining planning permits and doing structural calculations to designing the fit-out of buildings and supervising their construction.

The fitting-out department even tested and produced the acoustic finishing of the school's auditorium. Bauhaus students were also involved in designing and building the exhibition stands for the Gemeinnützige Aktiengesellschaft für Angestellten-Heimstatte in Berlin. For such jobs, the students jointly received 40 per cent of the design fee, which helped make architecture education affordable to working-class students.[12]

The experiment was short-lived, as was Hannes Meyer's directorship. The Bauhaus was forced to close its doors in 1933. The newly installed Nazi government deemed its products a form of deviant art and the school itself too communist.

Meyer's initiative remained an exception. After the Second World War, theory and practice continued being separate domains as before. Compulsory semesters of site work gradually disappeared from the curriculums of major universities and polytechnics, and in most architecture schools there was a dwindling interest in anything practical. A scan of the courses offered by architecture departments in American Ivy League universities is revealing of the trend. Harvard offers courses on Deleuze and Landscapes, on the Heterotopias of Bavarian Rococo, and one covering the spectrum from Minimalism to Neuro-phenomenology in Architecture and Art. Columbia GSAPP teaches a studio titled Provocations from Neuroscience, and Yale one titled Utopics: Utopias, Dystopias, Technotopias, and Heterotopias in Architecture and Urbanism, as well as multiple courses related to the concept of 'Storybuilding'.

Where the Bauhaus was political in that it was *for* something – that is, it endorsed a particular political ideology – contemporary education is invariably defined in terms of being *against* something. What exactly is being opposed remains ill-defined. Columbia GSAPP offers a course on the Architecture of Activism, and the Royal Danish Academy one on Political Architecture and Critical Sustainability. Insofar as there is definition, the colonial is a hot topic. Harvard GSD has a course called Coloniality, Subject, and Space, under the heading Other(ed) Architecture, while the MIT Department of Architecture has one called Decolonial Ecologies. Yale School of Architecture offers one called From Decon to Decolonial, featuring Peter Eisenman, as well as an Advanced Design Studio on De-Colonizing Indigenous Housing. TU Delft offers a course on Spatial Justice, UCLA one on Spatial Justice and the City, and the School of Architecture & Environment at the University of Oregon one on How to Design for Spatial Justice.

What activism is to political injustice, identity politics are to social injustice. At Harvard GSD, the Queer Home combines architecture with movement-based practice to speculate on the future of housing. At the AA, Queer Aided Design explores shared and plural sensibilities to centre the exchange of personal stories of queer spaces and space making within and outside of architecture schools. At Princeton, a seminar on Gender, Cities and Dissent investigates how eco-feminism and intersectional feminism as well as queer and trans theory can spearhead new ways of seeing and analyzing spaces, buildings and cities, as well as the human alliances within them.

And then (of course) there is placemaking – a word with no dictionary definition that has managed to galvanize public policymakers and educators alike. Harvard offers a course called Plants and Placemaking, Pratt Institute one on Urban Placemaking and Management, and University College of Dublin one on Placemaking, Urban and Rural. The University of New England has Placemaking for the People and the Environment, while Monash University teaches Gender-Sensitive Training for Inclusive Placemaking.

Increasingly, the intellectual climate at architecture schools feels like a self-imposed theatre of the absurd. The subjects taught defy comprehension and, in most cases, seem selected based on an inversely proportional relation to their relevance in the real world. Even the idea that architecture schools should prepare for practice has become controversial. Once a vehicle to delay entering practice, contemporary architecture education increasingly offers the possibility of avoiding it altogether.

Take the recent proliferation of PhDs. They can be granted only by universities, but the criteria to be met in applying for one are meagre without exception. A master's degree, sometimes even a bachelor's, suffices. Good grades are optional. No work experience is required. PhDs are meanwhile the standard career path for most teachers in architecture schools. Conversely: most teaching jobs require a PhD. This closed-loop system has made PhDs a viable, self-perpetuating business. As a candidate, you get to prolong student life while earning more than you would as a recent graduate working in an architecture office; as a school, PhD programmes offer you access to grants that would otherwise be off limits.

A PhD in architecture implies doing research. The question is: research on what? The absurdity of the courses offered at universities is also reflected in their PhDs: TU Eindhoven has one titled Digital Placemaking and Healthy Ageing; the University of Huddersfield has one on Drawing as Placemaking; the University of Leeds one on Modernity & Gender Spaces; at UPenn, a PhD has been done titled Blurring Binaries and

Bending Gender: An Architecture of Love, and at the University of Cambridge there has been one on Architecting Hippocampal Plasticity through Spatial Complexity. In the early twenty-first century, the idea of architecture education and the idea of educating architects have become two very different things.

Meanwhile the world turns. With or without architects. Already, more than 90 per cent of all buildings are produced without an architect being involved. And the number is steadily on the rise. The more it happens, the more the fundamental redundancy of the architecture profession in its current form is exposed. What we have come to regard as skilled labour is precisely the type of labour that has come to embody a manifest absence of skills. The incidental charming initiative of having students build their own timber pavilions in public parks has little or nothing to do with prevailing modes of building. Alberti's imagined rhetorical supremacy of the architect meets its Waterloo in the realities of twenty-first-century construction.

That battle is increasingly evidenced in the conditions under which architecture is practised. The discipline that once actively sought to distance itself from brick and mortar is now the underlying party. Architects earn less than bricklayers. And the wage gap isn't limited to bricklayers. In the UK, Part 1 and Part 2 architectural assistants earn £23,000 and £30,000 per year respectively (2022),[13] whereas a skilled subcontractor earns £37,000 (2023).[14] In the Netherlands, the average architecture salary is €33,000 (2024).[15] Meanwhile, an unskilled construction worker earns €34,000 and a skilled one €36,000 (2024).[16]

Half a millennium after Alberti, the distinction between mental and manual labour in the construction industry is ever present. Architects count as doing the former, the workforce of the contractor as doing the latter. The conditions once thought exclusively applicable to the latter – low wages, long hours, and the fight against them – have equally come to apply to the former, if not more so. If in the 1920s architects still frowned at the thought of forming labour unions, they might today be thinking again.

However, rather than drawing petty comparisons between the rewards for mental and manual labour, and insisting on the superior nature of the first, it might be worth observing the unfavourable position of both, that is, the position of labour as a whole. In 'the economy of building', the labour involved in the design and execution of buildings has come to represent but a negligible portion of the total proceeds made from building. By far the largest portion goes to the sale (and resale) of buildings themselves – to real estate investment advisors, property investment consultants, financial consultants, private equity managers, capital markets advisors, corporate finance advisors, mergers and acquisitions lawyers, tax lawyers, zoning and land use lawyers, environmental law consultants, transaction advisors, real estate negotiators, debt financing advisors, equity financing advisors, real estate syndication advisors, real estate market research analysts, risk management consultants, real estate strategy consultants and real estate performance analysts.

The same disparity between the remuneration of architects and bricklayers applies in the extreme when comparing either to any of these professions. With earnings ranging between £40,000 and £100,000 per annum (not including bonus payments), the financial compensation of the average real estate agent far outdoes that of architects or construction workers, and more often even that of the two combined.

This disparity in earnings speaks volumes. In the economy of building, both the architect and the contractor are short-changed. They carry the bulk of the effort, and assume most of the risks, yet their labour is a negligible source of reward.

In the fight for a fairer distribution of rewards, architects and construction workers are ultimately on the same side. It's time to face reality: architects are working class – pure and simple. University degrees or not. If indeed the education of architects is to be political, it is *that* realization that needs to be at the core. Instead of focusing on perceived injustices to fight *against*, the recalibration of the building economy – and with it the just reward for labour invested – is the one compelling cause to fight *for*.

Architecture education is still a long way off. In ignoring the elephant in the room and promoting all sorts of invented causes instead, it unwittingly contributes to the erosion of the profession on a daily basis. In its present form, academia is the great smokescreen – a lethal cocktail of misplaced self-importance and narcissistic pseudo-activism.

Come to think of it, there is a curious resonance between the abstract subject matter of so-called 'architecture' courses at leading universities and the abstract job titles of those in the real estate trade. The indignation of the one curiously mirrors the delight of the other. Neither seems to have any real interest in changing the nature of the built environment itself – a reliable source of financial extraction for one, and a topical scapegoat for society's failings for the other.

Conveniently, the two hardly ever cross paths. If they do meet, in the context of conferences or symposia, the abstract nature of their language forever prevents any difference in position from manifesting itself. They politely share the stage as 'false friends'. If only because any real crossing of swords would spell the end of the business model of both. Lucrative or lamentable . . . even if contrary, the verdicts of business and academia on the built environment ultimately serve the same aim.

It is time to remove architecture education from its ivory tower. Hardly an original statement perhaps. And not a very radical one either. Yet, the very fact that something so obviously not radical comes to qualify as a radical proposition is indicative of how badly things have gone off track. When the obvious needs arguing, when false consciousness causes one to act against one's own interests, the need to recalibrate is a given.

Time for shock therapy!

End the distinction between theory and practice. Make working on a construction site a compulsory part of architectural education – mandatory for both students and teachers, required for the former to graduate and for the latter to qualify. Not because either needs to master 'the craft of building' or learn about 'brick and mortar' per se, but because both urgently need to be exposed to a reality that they have been allowed to look away from for too long.

Let's stop seeing architects for what they are not; let's recognize them for what they are, and, from there, imagine what they *could* be. Let's reinvent the architect as a working-class hero, standing shoulder to shoulder with concrete workers, plumbers, pipefitters, bricklayers, tile setters, welders, roofers, electricians, crane operators. Let's forge a common bond, enacted on construction sites, with the power to make run, or to stop, the tools of production.

A union between architects and construction workers could be the basis of a revolution, not just in the construction industry, but in society as a whole – a tactical and necessary step in the overall rehabilitation of labour and its reward. This revolution cannot be taught; it must be 'lived'. Architects need to get their hands dirty. Lofty architectural theories must be exorcised. No more opium for the educated!

Go! Flourish in the field. No more and no less than one year. Put on your hard hat, wear your 'gilet jaune', lace up your steel-toe boots. Accept the instructions you're given. Quietly go about your work. Take pride in every brick that is laid, in every window installed, in every new floor that is completed. All the while, never forget who you are! Cherish the anger towards those who unjustly reap the rewards of your labour. Nurture that anger! Let it fuel the courage you need to overthrow those who have expelled you to the margins and are about to condemn you to poverty. Arise ye architects from your slumber!

II

Architecture

8

Faux Arts

Architecture is the mother of all arts.[1] Architecture is art, and art is architecture; both are expressions of the human spirit.[2] Architecture is a thing of art, a phenomenon of the emotions, lying outside questions of construction and beyond them.[3] Architecture is art, but vastly contaminated by many other things. Contaminated in the best sense of the word – fed, fertilized by many things.[4] Architecture is the art of bringing people together, of creating places where communities can thrive.[5] What I try to do is the art of building, and the art of building is the art of construction; it is not only about forms and shapes and images.[6] Architecture is about trying to make the world a little more like our dreams.[7] I don't think architecture is about only shelter, is only about a very simple enclosure. It should be able to excite you, to calm you, to make you think.[8] I believe architecture is a pragmatic art.[9] The purpose of construction is to make things hold together; of architecture to move us.[10] I have tried to get close to the frontier between architecture and sculpture and to understand architecture as an art.[11] The ultimate goal of the architect . . . is to create a paradise.[12] Architecture is an art when one consciously or unconsciously creates aesthetic emotion in the atmosphere and when this environment produces well-being.[13] If architecture were not art, it would be astonishingly easy to build houses.[14] Architecture is art, nothing else.[15]

Is architecture art? The more emphatic the insistence, the less convincing the supposition becomes. Probably the most compelling case for why architecture is not art can be made simply by listing the prolific statements claiming that it is – a mixed bag of pretentiousness and delusion.

The above statements, all made by architects, are indicative of the state of mind of a profession that feels deeply unacknowledged on its own terms. Architects consistently claim to be artists; the reverse (almost) never happens. The love affair between architecture and art is one-sided at best. And the more architecture pursues the love affair, the more it tends to put one off the type of people practising it. In real-life terms, architecture might be accused of being the art stalker. The more the stalker identifies with their prey, the more they lose sight of their own personality, ultimately ending up a societal outcast or, in the worst-case scenario, a convicted felon. Architecture is not art, nor should it try to be. Attempts to make it such are to the detriment of both architecture and architects.

The *Oxford English Dictionary* defines 'art' as: 1) the expression or application of human creative skill and imagination, typically in a visual form such as painting or sculpture, producing works to be appreciated primarily for their beauty or emotional power; 2) the various branches of creative activity, such as painting, music, literature, and dance. In both parts of the definition, 'creative' is the pivotal adjective. Among the creative activities listed in the second definition, architecture is not mentioned. In terms of semantics, the conclusion is unequivocal: architecture is not an activity, even less so is it creative; therefore, architecture is not art.

Still the equation persists. Understandably perhaps. The production of architecture undeniably requires skill, imagination – even vision – and can solicit emotional responses pretty much in the way art does. Like art, architecture can inspire awe, indifference and disgust. In that respect, there is plenty of room for confusion. Yet, regardless of the similarities attributed to them, there is one big difference: artists do things; architects are *asked* to do things. Even if both are historically dependent on patronage, the key difference resides in the nature of the initiative. In the case of the former it is solicited; in the case of the latter it is sanctioned. When commissioned, artists are generally asked to do the things they do; architects are more often asked to do the things they're told to do.

Where art may qualify as 'free expression', architecture is invariably triggered by others. As such, it is also forever answerable to others. Whatever additional aspirations architects may have, they are expected to put them second to the requirements they are expected to meet. Once commissioned, architects find themselves in a situation that is anything but free. They are consistently monitored – for their adherence to briefs, to laws, standards and regulations, or to whatever other set criteria they must comply with.

Lack of freedom is the very essence of architecture. It is what explains its manic will to freedom, as well as the status 'freedom' holds within architecture. That status, however, is very different to the status of freedom in art. Freedom in art is hardly a quest. Quite the opposite. What is a pursuit in the case of one (architecture) is a curse for the other (art). Art is haunted by a freedom it can never conquer, architecture by one it can never achieve. Where artists desperately look for clues, references or, better still, 'context' to 'ground' the unbearable lightness of their artistic freedom, architecture is obsessed with the reverse: a desperate search for freedom in a context of utter dependency. Just as artists forever talk about 'materiality' to escape the intangibility of their craft, architects forever talk about 'space' to escape the incorrigibly material nature of their trade. All that is solid must melt into air.

Architecture was part of the curriculum of the École des Beaux-Arts from 1671 to 1968 – the year a violent student revolution swept across France and changed the face of education forever. Until then, the school had offered instruction in architecture alongside drawing, painting, sculpture and engraving. The École's prestigious Prix de Rome was awarded for competence across all five disciplines.

Within the educational system of the École, no distinction was made between art and architecture. Taught according to clearly defined aesthetic imperatives, evolving through imitation, the arts were no more a form of free expression than architecture. In addition, there was no difference between art and architecture in terms of earning a living. Graduates in painting and sculpture were expected to live off commissioned work just as much as architecture graduates. The École's mission was to educate 'professionals in the arts' – to transfer from generation to generation the legacy of classicism and classical architecture as an acquirable set of skills.

It can be argued that the École lived most of its life on borrowed time. Roughly a century after its formation, the Industrial Revolution brought profound changes that affected – or rather, *should* have affected – its teachings. The school maintained its doctrines in the face of a world that had moved on, a world in which industrial production radically changed the nature of building, and processes of mechanical reproduction drastically affected the status of art. From an absolute, classicism became a style, and the preservation of its legacy a matter of competence more than conviction.

Not until the early twentieth century did the defining challenge become manifest. In the context of institutions like the Bauhaus (1919) and Vkhutemas (1920), architecture and art became the forefront (the avant-garde) of the search for a visual expression of a new world order. Both accelerated their journey towards abstraction. Reproductive technologies like photography and film had led art to gradually remove itself from the representational. Constructivism, Suprematism and De Stijl continued where Impressionism, Fauvism and Cubism had left off. Similarly, the introduction of reinforced concrete and the mass production of steel enabled architecture to abandon ornament and decoration.

The new world order hardly meant the end of the allegiance between art and architecture. While the latter had been just one of multiple art forms within the Beaux Arts, with the Bauhaus, architecture, or rather 'building', became the end goal of all the arts combined. 'The ultimate goal of all art is the building!', wrote Walter Gropius, outlining the school's mission.[16] The unassuming use of the term 'building' (in lieu of architecture) is misleading. The rejection of the term 'architecture' only served to escalate its centrality yet further. Gropius's idea of 'Total Architecture' was to architecture what the idea of Total Art (*Gesamtkunstwerk*) was to Richard Wagner's opera. In rejecting the Beaux Arts tradition, Gropius stealthily engineered its apotheosis. When it comes to totalizing ambitions for the arts, the Bauhaus is the École des Beaux-Arts on steroids.

The cases of both Gropius and Wagner signify the extent to which any mobilization of the arts towards a unified aim is dependent on political patronage. The École des Beaux-Arts had been sanctioned by the French king; Vkhutemas was the initiative of the newly formed communist regime in the USSR; the Bauhaus could only exist thanks to the progressive policies of the Weimar Republic; and Wagner was sponsored by King Ludwig of Bavaria – well before acquiring his legacy as Hitler's favourite muse.

After the Second World War, political patronage continued in a more sedate form. The welfare state relied on modern architecture (or derivates thereof) to provide most of its citizens with decent homes, and on modern art museums to gently coach the public into adopting the welfare state's generally progressive view of the world. As art became confined to the museum, architecture came to be equated, by default, with the production of mass housing. Ironically, the outcome of the industrial methods advocated by the Bauhaus was not the apotheosis of architecture as the goal of all art, but rather the seeming disappearance of architecture altogether.

Major changes seemed to present themselves with the advent of postmodernism in the late 1960s and early 1970s. Art and architecture acquired a new prominence, as did the echoes between them. Where postmodernism in art embraced irony and appropriation, postmodernism in architecture found its expression in an eclectic pastiche – first as a potpourri of historical styles, later also by alluding to modernism itself as a style.

Both art and architecture started to incorporate elements of popular culture and mass media. The fascination with popular culture in the work of an artist like Richard Hamilton is echoed in Robert Venturi's *Learning from Las Vegas*. Jeff Koons' kitsch-as-fine-art and Frank Gehry's turning of scrap materials into architecture serve as more recent examples. Even at the height of their combined fame, art and architecture remain firm in their countercultural reflexes. They seem closer than ever. It is telling that the most emphatic of the statements quoted at the start of this chapter – 'architecture is art, nothing else' – is from Philip Johnson, made in reference to Gehry's Guggenheim Museum in Bilbao.

While in historical terms it is tempting to view postmodernism as a critique of modernism's commonly accepted truths and hierarchies – in architecture by emphatically breaking with the prevailing ethos of modern architecture, in art by intentionally blurring the boundaries between high and low culture – there is also the point to be made that, precisely by undermining these accepted truths, postmodernism served as the ultimate legitimization of the system that came to succeed modernism.

By cultivating a scepticism towards grand narratives and rejecting the idea of a single artistic truth in favour of irony and fragmentation, postmodernism de facto came to align itself with the deregulatory, anti-collectivist ethos of the market economy. There is a fine line between attacking one power and enforcing the next. In presenting itself as an ideologically non-committal free-for-all, postmodernism provided the perfect cultural front for the dismantling of structures based on collectivity and solidarity such as the welfare state and labour movements. As postmodernism's most eminent forms of expression, art and architecture, knowingly or unknowingly, helped pave the way for the commodification of all aspects of life, including art and architecture themselves.

From being earnest proponents of the welfare state, art and architecture became intellectually conflicted agents of the market economy. Even if pillars of different powers, pillars they remained. Postmodernism going mainstream in the 1980s turned out to represent not so much a shift away from political patronage as a particular twist on it – one in which prevailing cultural expressions served the interests of power just as they had in previous epochs, but were just not as upfront about it. Postmodernism has been equally interpreted as a critical comment on the prevailing mores of the market economy and as an embrace of those mores. We will never know. Irony allows an endless deflection of the question.

More than forty years on, wondering about the cultural significance of postmodernism feels like little more than a lofty pastime. The historic significance of the 1980s only becomes truly apparent once we recount the period not in art-historical but in economic terms. Between 1981 and 1986, the prohibition on US banks holding interest-bearing demand deposit accounts was phased out as a result of the Depository Institutions Deregulation and Monetary Control Act of 1980. This prohibition had been in place since 1933 to limit risky, speculative behaviour by banks competing for customer deposits.

The deregulation allowed banks to channel vastly increased amounts of capital into speculative investments, including art and real estate. Art and architecture acquired a new patron in the form of capital, subject to favourable tax regimes, and more than once facilitated by new twists to old laws.[17]

The globalization that followed took things to the next level. In 1999, the US Financial Services Modernization Act, also known as the Gramm-Leach-Bliley Act, further removed barriers by allowing financial institutions to simultaneously act as any combination of investment bank, commercial bank and insurance company.

Both the art and real estate markets were propelled to unprecedented heights. In November 2013, the triptych *Three Studies of Lucian Freud* (1969) by Francis Bacon was sold by Christie's New York for $142.4 million to American billionaire and art collector Elaine Wynn. (After which she loaned it to the Portland Art Museum.) In May 2015, Pablo Picasso's *Les femmes d'Alger ('Version O')* (1955) was sold by Christie's for $179.4 million to former Qatari Prime Minister Hamad bin Jassim bin Jaber Al Thani. In May 2019, *Rabbit* (1986) by Jeff Koons was sold for $91.1 million by Christie's, the most expensive artwork by a living artist ever, until it was surpassed by the NFT artwork *The Merge* by Pak, which sold for $91.8 million on Nifty Gateway in December 2021.

What happened to art happened equally to architecture. Well-known buildings from the same period saw the same escalation in value: Mies' Seagram Building was built for $43 million in 1958, sold for $85.5 million in 1979, and designated an NYC landmark in 1989, after which the real estate investor Aby Rosen acquired a majority share in the building for $375 million in 2000. Another NYC landmark, the

AT&T Building by Philip Johnson, was built for $200 million in 1983. In 2002, its occupant Sony activated its option to buy the building for $236 million and then sold it to Chetrit Group in 2013 for $1.1 billion. In 2016, it was sold on to the Olayan Group for $1.4 billion. (A failed plan to convert it into condominiums would have brought in $1.8 billion.) In 2004, Swiss Re financed the construction of 30 St Mary Axe, also known as the Gherkin, by Foster + Partners, for £138 million. In 2007, the building was sold to German real estate group IVG Immobilien and UK investment firm Evans Randall for £630 million. In 2014, it was purchased for £700 million by the Safra Group, making it the most expensive office building in the UK to date.

The financial crisis of 2008 could have changed the world forever – and the world of real estate in particular. It didn't. Seventeen years on, thanks to their proven potential for appreciation, art and buildings count among the best and safest investments possible – a hedge against inflation within the portfolios of pension funds, sovereign wealth funds or simply wealthy individuals. At a 2015 conference in Singapore, then BlackRock CEO Laurence Fink stated that the two greatest stores of wealth internationally were contemporary art and apartments in Manhattan, Vancouver and London. The facts backed him up: that same year, Christie's art sales equalled $1 billion in a single week, while the median sale price of a Manhattan condo jumped to $1.3 million.

In economic terms, buildings, like artworks, are an 'asset class'. In Marxist theory, assets (or commodities) are subject to two types of value: use value and exchange value, which exist independently of each other. What they share is the labour embodied in them. However, where use value presumes a certain proportionality to the labour invested – a car is more expensive than a kitchen sieve – exchange value exists independently of labour. Something is worth whatever somebody is willing to pay for it. The difference between the amount received from selling it and the cost of manufacturing it qualifies as 'surplus value', the maximization of which constitutes the core of the capitalist system as well as the most important object of its Marxist critique.

Surplus value is the excess of value produced over the cost of labour invested. The evolution of art plays an interesting role in this respect. Where traditional art may still be appreciated for the effort invested in it – a manifestation of apparent skill and training – modern art renders any such notion irrelevant. The labour invested in it is a non-issue. Any inquiry as to the hours invested in Malevich's *Black Square* qualifies as a vulgar question in the face of its otherwise sublime achievement – the end of art . . . only to propel the aura of all art to unprecedented levels.

'Nothing can have value, without being an object of utility. If the thing is useless, so is the labour contained in it; the labour does not count as labour, and therefore creates no value', Marx concluded in *Capital*.[18] Let's project this onto art. A work of art is not an object of utility; therefore, in theory, it has no value. The previously listed sales of artworks, however, present a decidedly different picture. The abstraction of modern art and the abstract nature of exchange value seem to meet in perfect sync. In obfuscating any relation between effort and effect, and thus between labour and value, art becomes the perfect carrier of surplus value.

Art is simultaneously everything and nothing. The lucrative nature of this ambiguity is evidenced in the record sale prices of artworks at auctions. Art comes to approach speculation in its pure form. All comprehension falters. The greater the number of curators and art critics to make sense of it all, the less we understand. 'L'art pour l'art' met its destiny in 'l'art contre l'art', until that, too, was exposed as a tiresome encore. In the end, only 'l'art' remained, explained by nothing, not even by itself. Contemporary art enjoys the right to remain silent. 'Untitled'. Take it or leave it.

Project the same mechanism onto architecture. Buildings sold for record profits, propelling ever newer, ever younger generations of architects to fame. Interchangeable signature styles, every single one as unique as the other. Titanium scrap heaps, pivoted cubes, fenestrated phalli, gravity-defying needles, and so on.

Sadly, this is not some dystopian (or perhaps utopian to some) future, but a pretty accurate snapshot of the contemporary real estate market. Like artworks, buildings have become a surplus category in the extreme. The figures mentioned earlier in this chapter are indicative. In each case, the value gained from trading far outstrips both the material and non-material costs of the investment.

It is interesting to analyze the relative share of labour in that investment. There are two things to observe here: development market value (typically the value of sale) and development cost. Both serve as a basis for the reward of associated labour. The development cost includes the following items: 1) land cost, 2) construction cost and 3) building services cost. Architects are usually paid between 5 and 10 per cent of the construction cost, depending on the *scale of the project*; contractors between 20 and 30 per cent, depending on *project complexity*. After deducting expenses, architects usually keep 15 per cent of their earnings, in other words 0.75 to 1.5 per cent of the construction cost. Contractors usually keep 10 per cent, or 2 to 3 per cent of the construction cost. Developers, meanwhile, wouldn't even be talking to a bank if they didn't plan to pocket at least 16 per cent of the total development cost after selling the building. Banks, in turn, gain around 5 to 7 per cent on what they lend (as of 2024). The real estate agent in charge of the sale usually gets between 1 and 2 per cent of the sale value.

Applying the above numbers to the Gherkin, with a construction budget of £138 million, the architect, Foster + Partners, would have made a profit of £1.03 million, the contractor, Skanska, £4.14 million, the bank, unspecified, £5.5 million, the agents, advisors and consultants, DTZ and Eurohypo, £6 million. Estimating total development costs at £328 million, the developer, Swiss Re, would have cashed in roughly £272 million when it sold the building to IVG Immobilien for £630 million in 2007.[19] All profits combined, the profit to the architect ends up being no more than 0.35 per cent. Meanwhile, the building has been sold once more, to Brazilian billionaire Joseph Safra for £726 million.[20]

Buildings cost money; buildings earn money. The latter barely registers on the radar of architects. Even the high fees commanded by a practice like Foster's bear no relation to the surplus value created by their products. Foster may consider himself one of the lucky ones. For most architects, the reality of escalating sales prices and ever more expensive real estate has coincided with ever dwindling fees. The conception of buildings as art, and the subsequent trailing of the economy of art, benefits only the happy few, and, in the end, not even them. The starving artist: a long-outdated concept in art; an increasingly pressing reality for architects.

The economy of architecture firms aside, the primacy of exchange value has a significant effect on architecture itself. The gradual withdrawal of use value as a paradigm signals the end of architecture – or, more plainly, of buildings – as utilities. It is as though the twenty-first century has given Gropius's adage that 'the goal of all art is the building' a sardonic twist: 'the goal of all building is (to be) art'. Architecture becomes synonymous with museums that openly compete with the art collections displayed in them; more often still, with museums that house no collection at all, libraries that contain no books, stores with nothing for sale, and endless, endless volumes of empty residential real estate.

This last category is affecting our cities and (any possibility of) life within them. Already, most city centres have become far too expensive places to live for most people. The fraught equation of architecture and art finds its apotheosis not in the Guggenheim Bilbao, but in the artistry of the unoccupied ultrathin residential tower. Taking its inspiration from a trash can designed by Josef Hoffmann, the unoccupied residential tower represents exchange value in its purest form – there not to be used, but to be owned and traded, exemplary of how, in its terminal stage, the annexation of architecture by capital requests even the exorcism of the human condition.

The equation with art turns architecture into a dog chasing its own tail, reinventing itself every decade, every year, every month, every week, with every new Instagram post. Ever greater are the postures of extravagance, the invocation of 'genius' and the unrelenting faith in cure-all solutions. Architects are miracle workers, their works coveted by aspiring politicians, museum directors and corporate moguls alike, offering an infinitely renewable cycle of hope to each. Institutions, cities, sometimes entire nations pin their hopes on a single masterpiece. The greater the hopes pinned on a specific building, the greater the feeling of being let down by buildings in general. The more that is attributed to architects, the more architecture disappoints.

A giant sculpture greets visitors in front of the Guggenheim Museum Bilbao – *Puppy*, a behemoth West Highland terrier carpeted in bedding plants. According to the artist, it is there to instil 'confidence and security'.[21] The bedding plants are a reference to eighteenth-century formal European gardens, the sort everyone likes. The artist is known to have a thing for popular culture. As did the architect of the museum – once. Raw, off-the-shelf industrial materials like corrugated metal and chain-link fencing typified his early works: casually assembled structures with no apparent regard for formal order, the kind lay people might have built. But that was a long time ago. These days his buildings are credited with unparalleled powers, larger than life, or at least larger than the cities that host them.

The casual disregard for his own profession has become hard to maintain, as has the burden of attempting to repeat 'the effect' attributed to his creations over and over again. The Bilbao museum has welcomed over 25 million visitors and is estimated to have generated 7.7 billion euros in revenue for the city. Twenty-five years on, the building looks tired and worn, grey as the autumn sky above it, as if somehow exhausted from its own efforts. *Puppy* is still there, colourful and uplifting. No calculations have been made as to its contribution to the effect. There is no 'Puppy effect'. If there were, Puppy would probably dismiss it in good spirit. Art endures only the obligation to be art.

All wishful thinking notwithstanding, the same cannot be said of architecture, from the education of architects as 'professionals in the arts' at the École des Beaux-Arts, to art being at the service of architecture in Gropius's Bauhaus, to their joint participation in today's 'aura economy'. The longer and more emphatically we insist on their combined potential, the more we seem to facilitate the abuse of both. Architecture inevitably draws the short straw. The more we regard buildings as works of art, the more they are forced to behave as such – as the unwitting agents of global capital, complicit in stratospheric returns and catastrophic losses. The elusive disclaimers that apply to art – irony, the imitation of life – will never apply to architecture in the same way. Irony in architecture is a losing proposition. Buildings were the pillar of a speculative economy without guardrails that brought the world to the brink of a financial abyss in 2008. No excuse to date has got them off the hook. The equation of architecture with art is more precarious than ever. It is time to file for divorce.

9

For Us, By Us

'I authorize you to put your theories into practice and to carry them to their most extreme conclusions; I wish to achieve really conclusive results in the field of low-cost housing: The project must be regarded as a laboratory. I authorize you to break with all conventions and abandon traditional methods!'[1] The architect is all too confident. He may not be that much of a known quantity yet, but the way he has just paraphrased the instructions of his client leaves little doubt as to what he considers to be his mandate: carte blanche!

That may not necessarily be the way his client sees it:

> I had told him: 'do it your own way', but what I had imagined was a garden city on a larger scale. The site was an extensive area of meadowland surrounded by a pine forest, famous for the pure air of its pine trees. I wanted to include gardens around each villa . . . Flowers everywhere, including the terraces . . .

> I had expressed a desire for the greatest possible variety in the designs, and that no two villas would be the same. But he [the architect] soon persuaded me that this view was exaggerated. The diversity which I wished to achieve had to be reconciled with the need for serial production, since this was the only way of reducing costs to any appreciable extent. Homes would have to be broadly identical in form and appearance. He suggested we adopt the principle of the game of 'patience' and 'lotto', allowing various fixtures to be joined together or separated as desired by the householder. A modular system of white boxes, to be placed in different arrangements, would allow for the necessary diversity . . .
>
> Painting the facades of the villas in different colors was the only concession I could extract from him. On the issue of decoration, I asked him to put himself in the place of the future purchasers, whose eyes are accustomed to decorative effect, even if of the most discreet kind. But he insisted that we leave the walls unfinished to the point that they still showed the marks of the shuttering. He told me that if we wished to offer the houses to the public at the lowest possible price we could not afford to spend money on unnecessary luxuries. He then launched into a diatribe against ornamentation, exclaiming: 'we are tired of decor, what we need is a good visual laxative! Bare walls, total simplicity, that is how to restore our visual sense!'[2]

The project described here is 100 years old, but the dynamic feels all too familiar: an architect moulding the will of his client into his own. Serious misalignments are ironed out in the name of a common purpose. Familiar, too, is the problem at hand: the client is not the user and therefore the purpose is only common insofar as the client is inclined to speak on behalf of future users, and capable of doing so. He is a delegate representative, funding a project for voiceless others. Concerning their wishes, he has a choice: he can either pretend to be all-knowing or confess to being unknowing. Either way, he has no leg to stand on.

The project in question is Cité Frugès in Pessac; the client recounting his memories is the French sugar industrialist Henri Frugès. Cité Frugès was intended to house employees of a packing-case factory owned by Henri's father. It is one of the first ever built social housing projects. The architect is the then unknown Le Corbusier.

Henri Frugès' recollections about his interactions with Le Corbusier date from July 1967, at an event organized by the town council to celebrate the fortieth anniversary of the project. By that time, Le Corbusier had been dead for two years. Whether prompted by that or not, his one-time client took ample license to speak freely, not just about their relationship, but also about the less-than-flattering opinions the project attracted from the general public. The inhabitants of Bordeaux, for one, hated it. They imagined the buildings were harems, as their closest point of reference for a terraced house was North Africa. Common nicknames for the development were 'the Moroccan Settlement' or 'the Sultan's District'. Or, given the nature of Frugès' business, 'Frugès' sugar cubes'.

Even more unambiguous was the verdict of the project's inhabitants: 'It's the sort of thing the Marabouts would have over in Africa . . . the pergolas, what use are they? . . . it would have been better to have fixed up a couple of extra rooms in a hut . . . rather than have that thing hanging up there [the terrace].'[3] 'When the windows were the full width of the house the youngsters next door used to amuse themselves by teasing the children we had here . . . so we blocked the window off . . . and then we put this single window in the centre, I prefer it like that.'[4] 'The windows aren't very pretty, are they? Why not? Well, because they're ugly!'[5] 'The terrace, like the veranda, serves no practical purpose, so we've gradually come to use it for storage, we put out . . . things, old things, old furniture.'[6] 'That man is completely mad . . . placing a chimney in the middle of the dining-room.'[7]

It didn't take long for inhabitants to put words into action. *Fenêtre en longueurs* were either blocked off or replaced by narrower windows punctuating the facades; most of the original terraces were roofed over, the empty spaces beneath the stilts were blocked off, verandas were repurposed as storage spaces, and the exterior walls of most of the houses were painted a different colour to the original. By the time of Frugès's speech, successive modifications by the inhabitants had changed the project's intended look and feel beyond recognition.

It was not until 1973 that one of the houses in Cité Frugès was restored to its original state. It was listed as a historic monument in 1980, the year when the Cité was also included in the Department's inventory of picturesque sites. In 1983, the city of Pessac itself bought one of the houses, which it restored in 1986 and opened to the public a year later. In 1998, the area was listed as a ZPPAUP (Zone de protection du patrimoine architectural, urbain et paysager – architectural, urban and landscape heritage protection zone), and in 2016 it was listed as a UNESCO heritage site under the title 'The Architectural Work of Le Corbusier, an Outstanding Contribution to the Modern Movement'. The buildings are described as 'masterpieces of creative genius [that] attest to the internationalization of architectural practice across the planet'.[8]

Clearly, both the extent and the early onset of Cité Frugès's modification constitute a serious challenge to any attempt at restoration. In confronting this challenge, the policies formulated by the ZPPAUP are ambiguous at best:

> From the start we believed that, in principle, the alternative was not between keeping everything or destroying everything – that is to say, between a reconstitution faithful to the original state or a renunciation of any intervention – but that there existed room for manoeuvre in which relevant architectural recommendations could be included, based on a simple theoretical framework allowing the preservation of this historic ensemble, while retaining its character as a 'popular residential city'.

In practice, this meant that only those homes that had undergone the least amount of modification (and had retained their original colours: twenty-eight out of fifty) were eligible to be officially listed as monuments. The burden on these homes is substantial. As the ZPPAUP document put it: each home ought to 'restore the visual and aesthetic appearance of the exterior works'.[9] Once again, they are to reflect Le Corbusier's five points: 1) the pilotis, 2) the roof gardens, 3) the *plan libre*, 4) *fenêtre en longueurs* and 5) the *facade libre*. The homes that have been modified beyond the point of no return are subject to a far less stringent regime. Apart from a recommendation to restore the 'polychromy' of the exterior walls, they can remain as they are for the time being. Here, the focus is on improving 'the overall image of the city' by restoring the original road and pavement surfaces, vegetation and street lighting.[10]

The ZPPAUP approach can be summed up as an opportunistic mix of intervention where possible, guardianship where tenable and laissez-faire whenever things are deemed beyond repair. Interesting, too, is the degree to which ZPPAUP restoration policies rely on the participation of the area's inhabitants, the objective of the listing being 'to safeguard this homogeneous and exemplary urban ensemble while involving its inhabitants, motivating them and raising their awareness of reasoned restoration, rehabilitation and renovation actions'.[11] Ironically, the process of restoring Le Corbusier's original intentions comes to depend on the exact same group that had done its utmost to annul them.

Public sector bodies presiding over the restoration effort seem all too aware of this. Inhabitants who want to restore their houses can apply for financial support. Between 2018 and 2021, a total of €183,000 was paid for seven work files submitted by private owners, ranging from simple repairs to comprehensive renovation projects. In 2021 alone, €93,000 was handed out. In 2023, the aid stopped.

Today, the house restored in 1986 needs to be restored again. The estimated cost is €840,000.[12] In 2016, an appeal for restoration funding was launched. In exchange patrons would receive a miniature of the house, an invitation to the inauguration and a 66 per cent tax deduction of the donated amount.[13]

In the end, in the attempt to resurrect everything that its architect might have intended, Cité Frugès becomes exemplary of the ambivalent, if not cynical, relationship that has come to exist between modern architecture and its users. In

Pessac, that relation has come full circle. In a desperate plea to help save the architect's views, city authorities resort to a fund-raiser, seeking financial support from those whose views the architect chose to ignore.

Cité Frugès is exemplary of the relation between modern architecture and modern architects on the one side, and their clients and users on the other – even when the latter two have been one and the same. It is telling that the two twentieth-century homes most revered by architects – the Villa Savoye and the Farnsworth House – were never properly occupied by their patrons and both ended up in litigation. In ignoring the user, Cité Frugès unwittingly demonstrates the centrality of the user – perhaps evidenced most clearly in the statement Le Corbusier made when confronted with the modifications in Pessac: 'It is life that is always right and the architect who is wrong.'

Historically, the moral claim of modern architecture in relation to housing is the discovery of its relevance. In a conversation with architecture students in 1943, Le Corbusier lamented the absence of housing as a formal part of the curriculum of the École des Beaux-Arts in Paris, posing his own approach as an antidote: 'In 1920, when we created *L'Esprit Nouveau*, I established the fundamental significance of the home by describing it as a "machine to live in" . . . An exclusively human programme, placing man once again in the centre of architectural creation . . . when it is devoted to dwellings, architecture is an act of love, not a *mise en scène*.'[14]

From a moral claim to a moral right is but a small step. For Le Corbusier, 'the centrality of man' is an abstract conception. Whether or not the architect's love is reciprocated is of no importance. In maintaining to be the only movement in architecture that was really interested in housing, modern architecture became the default expert on housing needs and thus the only legitimate mouthpiece of everyone in need of housing. The famous slogan 'architecture or revolution' is all about housing: the prevention of social unrest through housebuilding at the largest possible scale, the type Le Corbusier and his kindred spirits were ready to provide. Engage us, or else.

And who could argue with them? Since the Industrial Revolution, building or commissioning one's own home had been a privilege of the happy few. The provision of large amounts of housing by third parties was commonplace. Housing developments on land owned by wealthy industrialists, like Cité Frugès, were by no means exceptional. It was unusual for inhabitants to be asked for, or to convey, their wishes in advance. If they spoke at all, it was after the event, in the form of action, through the subtle (and sometimes not so subtle) process of appropriating their homes with the passing of time.

The Second World War, and the massive housing shortage that followed, took things to the next level. Housing became mass housing. Mass housing presumed the existence of 'the masses': anonymous pools of tenants defined in numbers only, united by a single need – a dwelling. In the context of the welfare state, large, state-run housing projects became the norm, relying heavily on industrialized building systems and the assembly of prefabricated concrete. In these circumstances, many of their architects were as anonymous as the masses they catered to.

For a while it worked. By the mid-1970s, housing shortages – not just in France, but in most European countries – had become a thing of the past. However, as the trend spread, so did the resistance. Having emphatically aligned itself with the issue of mass housing, modern architecture was now unforgivably linked to the anonymous housing estates produced in the wake of that alignment, synonymous with boredom and alienation.

Rent strikes occurred in multiple European countries, with residents protesting against everything from the lack of recreational facilities to changes to rent rebate schemes. Resident organizations were also created to resist the relocation of former inner-city populations to the newly built high-rises, where poor maintenance and management by public authorities only added to the frustrations.

New housing policies were implemented. From large housing estates the focus shifted to the renewal of inner-city neighbourhoods. Thus, the anonymous masses of the 1960s became the neighbourhood communities of the 1970s. The associated reduction in numbers made it possible to consult users with regard to their living environment. (Or for users to raise objections if they weren't properly consulted.) The idea of residents' participation developed in this period partly served as a reaction against the uniformity created by the welfare state during the decade before.

Residents' participation also implied the return of certain elements of pre-industrial practice. Once again, users could express their wishes, albeit that in most cases the architect was bound only to the extent that the commissioner endorsed those wishes. This half-baked involvement was frustrating both for users and architects, and is probably responsible for the negative connotations the idea of user participation continues to have today, again both for users and architects.

Resistance among architects themselves had been brewing since the early 1950s. In 1953, at the 9th International Congress of Modern Architecture (CIAM), disagreement over CIAM's overly technocratic stance led to the formation of the breakaway group Team X. In 1959, following Le Corbusier's exit from CIAM, Team X became its de facto successor. The group, which included influential figures such as Jaap Bakema, Georges Candilis, Giancarlo De Carlo, Aldo van Eyck, Alison and Peter Smithson, and Shadrach Woods, called for a renewed focus on 'the human' as the defining measure of architecture, and for attention to non-Western forms of living. In *The Otterlo Circles*, a conceptual drawing produced for the occasion, Aldo van Eyck aimed to promote a new synthesis between pre-war avant-garde architecture, classical architecture and the architecture of non-Western cultures – the so-called 'vernacular of the heart'.

Team X was by no means the only group of architects craving an alternative to the rigidity of modern planning. Since the late 1950s, John F. C. Turner had been studying informal settlements in Peru, while Bernard Rudofsky's 1964 exhibition at MoMA, *Architecture without Architects*, planted seeds of doubt about the architect's expertise altogether. In Belgium, Lucien Kroll, together with students at the Catholic University of Louvain (UCL), designed and built La Mémé, a housing project completed in 1976 on the outskirts of Brussels.[15] In Italy, Giancarlo De Carlo pioneered user participation with the Nuovo Villaggio Matteotti project, completed in 1975. In the UK, Walter Segal promoted self-building. In Portugal, the post-fascist government introduced a programme that connected architects with people in acute need of housing: SAAL (Serviço de Apoio

Ambulatório Local). One of the young architects involved was Álvaro Siza.

In the Netherlands, N. John Habraken developed a building system expressly aimed at encouraging interaction with users. Between 1975 and 1981, Habraken was the head of the Department of Architecture at MIT. In 1981, he published a text on participation in architecture and the new role of the architect, drawing attention to the initiatives of dwellers outside the purview of architects:

> The initiatives I referred to have always come into operation when dwellers and dwelling found each other. The old houses left to us from the past bear witness to this. Each generation, each occupant, changed what he found . . . These alterations were not always done for functional purposes. They were done to keep up with the times or because notions about living changed, because one could not identify with what one took over or because it belonged to a different generation.[16]

The link to Cité Frugès here is interesting: what happened by chance in Pessac became an express purpose in the context of Habraken's proposed method.

Perhaps the most eloquent proponent of user participation during this period was Giancarlo De Carlo, who advocated not just a different role for architects, but the gentle relinquishing of their totalizing mandate altogether:

> I don't think it is important to offer architecture an escape from its ancient dilemma between technology and art. Nor does it seem important to guarantee a role for architects by

> offering them a choice between being technicians and artists. In reality, the prospect which seems very interesting to me is that of taking architecture away from the architects and giving it back to the people who use it.[17]

At the same time, De Carlo was sceptical (realistic perhaps) about the extent to which his ideas might prevail:

> The political powers, including the Left, doubt the validity of the architecture of participation because they fear it; it extends the use of criticism and stimulates direct intervention, putting into question the fixed principle of delegation once and for all.[18]

In hindsight, that latter statement by De Carlo may have served as an ominous premonition. User participation as a theme in architecture was short-lived, topical only during a narrow window of time in the 1960s and '70s, bracketed by the eroding grip of the welfare state and the reliance on the free market that followed.

Once again, users slipped into the background. In the context of a liberalized, speculative housing market, they primarily exist as 'prospective buyers' – an unidentified group of people as incognito as the voiceless tenants before them. No longer were new projects subjected to painful interrogation in smoke-filled rooms. They either sold or they didn't. It was 'the market' that came to pass judgement.

But who is the market? No one can credibly claim to know the wishes of future users – neither property developers nor the architects working for them – simply because in a system rooted in speculation there *is* no way of knowing these wishes.

If, fifty years ago, housing developments were still produced in response to actual demographic necessities, today they must attract the populations they are intended for. No longer are the masses to be accommodated – they must be seduced.

'Landmark Living', 'Luxury All Around', 'Service with a Lifestyle', 'New Heights', 'Upscale', 'Head-turning Style', 'Urban Energy', 'Space to Balance Life, Work and Play' . . . We are offered abundant choices, but 'consumer choice' has hardly spelled the end of a monotonous built environment. All around we face the exact same products of the exact same slogans. The sum total of future users' preferences inevitably turns into an echo chamber filled with the vacuous marketing speak unleashed upon them.

The anonymous masses of the 1960s became the unknowable consumers of the 1990s. In acting as the self-appointed spokespeople of the former, modern architects unwittingly extended an open invitation to developers to become the sole proponents of the latter. Once primarily focused on housing, developers have become ubiquitous across the industry. Today, there is hardly a housing, office or retail project that unfolds without a developer. And their involvement doesn't stop there. Former public buildings, too, are being delegated to developers at lightning pace.

China's museum construction boom of the last decade has been handled entirely by real estate developers. In the US, multi-billion-dollar sports complexes are built by developers. Hospitals in the UK are built and managed by developers. In India, schools are built by developers through build-to-suit schemes. America's private prisons are designed, built and run by for-profit corporations. In the UK, developers get to build condominiums on church land in exchange for building new churches. In the US, churches have sold their properties to developers to raise cash and then rented them back. These days it seems there is no building type specific or bespoke enough not to have a developer involved.

The more developers take over, the more users recede into the background. Users stand to gain little from this situation, nor do architects. In the context of the paradoxical mechanics of a free market economy, it is increasingly unclear for whom and for what purpose buildings are produced. The more anonymous the users of buildings, the more emphatic the wishes that can be attributed to them. With no possibility of checking, architects are left defenceless. They become the passive recipients of a fictitious consensus, cornered by endless platitudes, forced to permanently second-guess what users might really want.

Users, in turn, only get to acquire a voice after purchase, manifesting their wishes by modifying their properties beyond recognition. Not that much has changed since the erection of Cité Frugès. In hindsight, Henri Frugès's biggest problem may have been not so much his inability to stand up to his architect as the fact that he was a middleman, just as the contemporary developer is a middleman, grandstanding between the wishes of his users and any possibility of the architect giving shape to them. Might things have been different if Le Corbusier had dealt directly with the prospective residents?

Once again, the user registers on the architect's radar. In the UK there is a renewed interest among architects in the self-building method of Walter Segal; Dutch architects, taking inspiration from Habraken, have launched the manifesto OpenBuilding.co; and a series of half-finished homes in Chile has propelled Alejandro Aravena to global fame.

The momentum isn't limited to architects. User participation in housing has a long civic tradition, and it is on the rise. Rising housing costs have made Germany's old concept of *Baugruppen* a mainstream alternative to traditional housing. Sweden's housing cooperatives go back to the late nineteenth century and make up almost a quarter of all housing today. The same applies to Switzerland. In Argentina, users have come to engage architects via *fideicomisos* – fiduciary contracts that enable the funding of projects from the collective assets of future users.

The economic effects are noticeable. In Germany, Baugruppen represent a 30 per cent cost saving versus developer-led housing schemes, while rents in Swiss housing cooperatives are on average 20 per cent lower than in private rental units. The same is true for Sweden.

Impressive as such effects may be, they remain volatile. Self-building tends to thrive in times of crisis, when market forces temporarily falter, only to be marginalized once the market picks up. In the period immediately after the crisis of 2008, the Dutch city of Almere relied heavily on its ambitious self-building programme to meet its housing quota, only to default to large property developers again once the crisis had passed. *Fideicomisos* came to prominence in Argentina shortly after the 2001 banking crisis and the large-scale withdrawal of private savings.

To become a plausible alternative to developer-led projects, self-building initiatives need to be embraced and promoted – not just in times of crisis but in a sustained fashion. And they need to be escalated both in scale and in scope. The same proliferation that has marked the world of property development must start to apply to self-building: it needs to become the default option for *all* types of building.

To achieve that, users will need to organize on a grand scale. Architects have a pivotal role to play here. Their all-round expertise in design, construction, cost and financing, and above all their knowledge of cities, puts them in a unique position to coordinate initiatives beyond the scale of the single user. Architects could reinvent themselves as the 'conveners' of 'user councils' – miscellaneous groups dedicated to the realization of anything from small housing developments to large residential complexes, from theatres and churches to shopping malls, from community centres and museums to sports facilities.

Leased land, borrowed capital, anonymous users. The unholy trinity that has hijacked the construction of our habitat must be broken. In reaping the returns from land it doesn't own, speculating with money it doesn't have, and acting on behalf of users it doesn't know, property development represents the ultimate empty vessel. It is an illusionist art that has magically convinced the world of its necessity. Since the invention of the skyscraper, it even involves the trading of air, literally.

No matter how highly architects think of themselves, in the speculative universe of commercial real estate the user and the architect are equally sidelined. The wishes of unknown users serve as a pretext to rein in the work of the architect; the whims of an absent architect serve as an alibi to deny users what they want. In snubbing the user, the architect only plays into the developer's hands. If architecture is to retain its legitimacy, it has no choice but to unreservedly reengage with those who use its products. It is time the architect and the user join forces and cut out the middlemen. Let's do what needs to be done.

10

Stop Building, Now!

On 17 August 2023, Chinese property developer Evergrande filed for protection from its creditors under Chapter 15 of the US Bankruptcy Code. A week later, Evergrande shares had plummeted by nearly 80 per cent. A last attempt to hand over majority control to Chinese banks and impose losses on foreign creditors was rejected in favour of an overall winding down of the company. A court-ordered liquidation in Hong Kong eventually followed in January 2024, and all trading of stocks in the China Evergrande Group was halted. After twenty-eight years, the second-largest property developer in China at the time, and the largest in the world in 2018 with a value of over £50 billion, was no more.

Why has every major economic crisis of the twenty-first century started with real estate? The 2008 global financial crisis was the result of a housing bubble, as was the later Eurozone housing crisis, as is China's current debt crisis marked by the fall of Evergrande. We are constructing more than any previous generation in history, only to discover that the line between our relentless urge to build and its total futility becomes ever finer. As more and more countries scramble to fund ambitious housing programmes, the modernist idea of an affordable home for all seems further away than ever. In the decade prior to the fall of Evergrande, China built more homes than the US did in the entire twentieth century. Many of them stand empty. Apart from the environmental cost, there is the cost to the plausibility of the system itself. As successive crises increasingly expose the true face of modern construction, fundamental questions arise about why we build in the first place. Are we trying to house people, or cash? The question touches the core of what architects do and why. If the legitimacy of a profession resides in the need for what it has to offer, then we will need architecture for as long as we need buildings. The question is: do we?

At the time of its liquidation in 2024, Evergrande had 1,300 projects in more than 280 cities across China. With the accumulation of development sites had come the accumulation of debt. This unfettered expansion regardless of the escalating financial risks is less exceptional than one might assume. A Chinese property bubble had been growing steadily since 2005. After the fiscal reforms of the 1990s, local governments were forced to cover a substantial part of the expenditure on their allocated infrastructure development. The 2008 financial crisis only exacerbated this trend, with local governments being made responsible for 70 per cent of the costs. As a result, they became ever more dependent on revenues from the land they owned. What followed was predictable: an indiscriminate selling of land-use rights to property developers.

The approach worked in part. By 2009, land values in China had tripled. Unfortunately, so had developer debts. By 2018, the central government had become so concerned that it announced it would not bail out creditors of bankrupt companies. This became official government policy in 2020, with Xi Jinping's so-called 'three red lines rule': the permissible debt of developers was to be determined according to three defining metrics: 1) their cash, 2) their equity and 3) their assets. After two decades of unfettered construction, the Chinese authorities had finally started to rein in the real estate market.

Evergrande was the first casualty. Just like Lehman Brothers in the US, it was long believed that Evergrande was too big to fail. Just like Lehman Brothers, it crashed. It had crossed each of Xi's three red lines, its fate an example of the newly enforced Chinese Communist Party creed that 'property is to be lived in, not speculated on'.[1]

Estimates of the number of empty homes in China vary. According to data from the country's National Bureau of Statistics, at the end of August 2023 the combined floor area of unsold homes stood at 648 million square metres. Based on an average home size of 90 square metres, that would be equal to 7.2 million empty homes, roughly 17.5 per cent of China's total stock. According to Goldman Sachs, the vacancy rate for urban residential property in China is even higher at around 20 per cent. And those numbers only include the number of homes left unsold. Including homes sold but not lived in has led to the dazzling estimation that China's empty stock could provide housing for over a billion people. As recently as September 2023, He Keng, a former deputy head of the National Bureau of Statistics, claimed that the total number of unfinished and finished-but-vacant apartment projects littered across China would be enough to accommodate in excess of the country's population of 1.4 billion.

'Ghost towns' were no longer places once inhabited but now abandoned; in China, the image of the ghost town became equated with cities where inhabitation had never taken place. As a response to a perceived demographic need, the planning of residential quarters amounted to a pre-emptive strike against masses that never came. The result was a pyramid scheme, in which the provision of homes became synonymous with the incurring of debt, to be paid off only by building yet more homes.

In 2009, Al Jazeera reported on the Inner Mongolian city of Ordos Kangbashi. Following various economic setbacks, Ordos's projected population of 1 million was successively scaled back to 500,000 and then 300,000 inhabitants. Of the apartments that were sold, few were lived in. Images of the city sent shockwaves around the world: stretches and stretches of shoulder-to-shoulder high-rise blocks, pristine but uninhabited, inserted into the landscape like a life-size model from the sales office.

Despite the lack of residents, the city went on to build prestigious projects such as the Ordos International Airport, the Ordos Museum, the Ordos Art Museum, the Ordos Library and the Ordos Sports Centre Stadium, with a capacity for 60,000 (absent) spectators. The development even included a scheme by Herzog & de Meuron and Ai Weiwei for 100 villas designed by 100 international architects. Today, just five exist in various stages of completion or abandonment.

Melissa Chan, the Al Jazeera journalist who first reported on Ordos, was expelled from China in 2012. But reports on the city had sufficiently highlighted China's vacancy rate for it to be officially recognized as a problem.

Recognition of the problem, however, hardly put an end to the practice itself. The main consequence was that Chinese developers started looking elsewhere. It was in Africa, with its massive demand for housing, that old ways found new fertile ground.

In 2008, a year before the Al Jazeera reports, Angola had launched an ambitious programme to build a million homes in four years. Thanks to its oil exports, the country had been enjoying steady economic growth since the end of the civil war in 2002. A net oil importer since 1993, China had been eager to develop commercial relations with oil-rich countries. A win-win situation presented itself. Millions of internally displaced Angolans were offered the prospect of a decent home, while China was able to export its construction industry.

To help finance the programme, a Chinese bank granted Angola an oil-backed loan worth around $6 billion. Work on the first of fifteen proposed new towns commenced in 2008: Nova Cidade do Kilamba, a city for half a million people, the largest new town in Africa.

In 2012, shortly after completion, Nova Cidade do Kilamba made global headlines as the surreal backdrop for a BBC broadcast about an African city for half a million people that stood completely empty.[2] In a country where two thirds of the population live on less than two dollars a day, and with no mortgage system, apartments labelled as 'social housing' costing between $120,000 and $200,000 seemed like a very bad joke.

The bulk of the apartments was eventually sold after Angola introduced a state-backed mortgage scheme, but most of them went to government employees or their friends, just as had happened earlier in Ordos. Other Angolan new towns have been completed meanwhile, further away from its capital, but it is unlikely, even for a country with a large bureaucratic apparatus like Angola, that all of them will be filled by government employees. With the current oil price at around half its 2008 value, neither the fate of Angola's economy nor that of its ghost towns seems very hopeful.[3]

Angola certainly isn't alone in having a vast stock of empty homes owned by people who don't need them and needed by people who can't afford them. When it comes to the provision of housing, the same paradox exists all over the African continent, with or without Chinese participation. In cities such as Lagos and Abuja in Nigeria, another oil-rich country, the lack of occupancy is generously compensated for by the higher rents paid by absent corporate executives, expatriates or other high earners. Add the depreciation from wear and tear arising from short-term rents and vacancy begins to look like a sound business strategy.

In South Africa, housing construction reached an all-time high after a sudden dip in interest rates at the onset of the COVID-19 pandemic reduced monthly mortgage instalments to the level of monthly rents. Two years later, a sharp rise in interest rates reversed the situation. The buyer's market evaporated and the country was left with a surplus of newly constructed homes. Its vacancy rate rose from 5 to 11 per cent.[4]

In Kenya, what looked like a nationwide property boom helped create a mismatch between real estate prices and average wealth levels from which the country is still recovering. The problem is not limited to empty residential properties, but also affects office buildings and shopping malls, with certain units remaining empty for over three years and increasingly larger discounts having no effect whatsoever.[5]

Accra, Ghana, represents a yet more extreme case. The appreciation in value of properties in the wealthier parts of the city, often owned by diasporic Ghanaians, has been such that even the need to rent them out has become obsolete. Vacancy in itself serves as an investment.[6]

There are over a million vacant homes in Morocco, almost all of them in urban areas. The vast majority were constructed within the last five years, most of them apartments, closely followed by villas. Traditional Moroccan houses account for less than 4 per cent of all vacancies.[7]

In Egypt, following an ambitious state-led push for affordable housing, official census data show that the total number of vacant housing units in the country has reached nearly 13 million units.[8]

To regard these excessive vacancy rates exclusively as a product of China, or of China exporting its methods to Africa would, however, be misguided. In 2014, 11 million houses stood empty in Europe, of which 700,000 were in the UK, 1.8 million in Germany, 2 million in France, 2 million in Italy, 3.4 million in Spain and roughly another million each in Portugal, Greece and Ireland.[9] In 2024 in the US, 15 million homes were estimated to be vacant, a large share of which were second homes.[10] In Buenos Aires in 2023, one-in-seven houses were empty as the country battled inflation,[11] while 11 million houses were vacant in Brazil, of which 6.6 million were holiday homes.[12]

Neither the recent fall of Evergrande nor the ongoing Chinese property crisis is an isolated phenomenon. Just as with the global financial crisis of 2008, they originate from the financialization of housing provision – a trend that has had consequences worldwide.

It can even be argued that the Chinese property crisis is a belated reaction to the crisis of 2008. There are certainly similarities. The 2008 crisis started in the US as a mortgage crisis resulting from predatory lending to low-income homebuyers. Following government legislation encouraging the financing of affordable homes, banks came up with a plethora of financial products, so-called 'subprime mortgages', to target low-income homebuyers. The type of market that ensued, unattended by regulators, took the entire US economy by surprise.

The Chinese property crisis unfolded roughly according to the same playbook: a government incentive to get the market to take over what had been a government task, followed by market forces going rampant, and finally the inevitable financial repercussions that come with a correction.

Owned but empty apartments have become an integral part of the fabric of any major city. Residences dark at night, ghost houses, sometimes entire quarters of them, can be found not just in China or Africa but throughout London, Paris and New York. The proliferation of unoccupied residential space also covers the full array of building types, from perimeter blocks in Spain to suburban tract homes in Florida. The exemplary instance is the empty residential skyscraper. Rafael Viñoly's 432 Park Avenue Tower is New York City's best-selling building ever, yet few of its apartment owners choose to take up permanent residence, and some of them have never even visited the place. With no residents present, its interiors are on permanent display. A home not for people but for money. New York City, meanwhile, has the highest homelessness rate since the Great Depression.

Prior to 2008, the presence of empty properties could be put down to investment miscalculation. Now,. real estate investment is in large part running on emptiness. Where vacancy used to be seen as a temporary condition that separated a building's present from its future, it is now viewed as an investment in a building's permanent present.[13] Where it used to be a problem to be solved by an investor, it is now treated as the solution to an investor's problems. In its terminal stage, the annexation of architecture by capital requires the exorcism of the human condition. As David Harvey put it in a 2016 lecture at Harvard Graduate School of Design: 'It seems that we are less and less interested in creating cities for people to live in. Instead, we are creating cities for people to invest in.'[14]

Housing shortages have been identified in practically every country of the world. But how real are they? Ambitious, state-incentivized construction programmes seem to coincide with massive vacancies in practically every place they are launched.

In Germany, the Scholz government pledged to build 400,000 homes per year from 2021, a doubling of the previous target. Perhaps unsurprisingly, the German government has been slow to deliver on this promise. With the construction industry plagued by rising interest rates and energy prices, the increasing cost of building materials and an acute shortage of skilled workers, just 245,000 apartments were built in 2023, and only 210,000 in 2025.[15] A graph showing housing completions over a ten-year period even reveals a slight drop after Scholz took office in 2021.[16] As things stand, Germany has a shortfall of over 800,000 apartments, with 9.5 million people living in cramped conditions.[17]

These numbers take on an interesting twist when one compares them with the country's vacancy rates. In 2022, a national survey revealed that nearly 2 million apartments in Germany stood empty – a vacancy rate of 4.3 per cent. Of these, more than half had been empty for at least a year, while a little more than a third, around 700,000, were available for occupancy within three months.[18] Just as in China, vacancy rates in Germany included brand new properties. Of those built after 2015, a good third (34 per cent) stood empty. In Hamburg and Berlin, the figure was around one in three (35 per cent and 29 per cent respectively), and in Saxony-Anhalt and Thuringia almost two thirds (64 per cent and 68 per cent). Nearly all the apartments had been empty for twelve months or more.

Moreover, it was found that on average only one in four apartments was empty because of ongoing construction or renovation work, with less than 14 per cent of all vacancy in properties built after 2015 attributable to such work. Contrary to what one might expect, the age of a property bears little to no correlation to vacancy.

In addition, Germany has witnessed a steady increase in empty office space, with a total of 2 million square metres of usable space vacant in the seven biggest office locations. Considering the average size of an apartment in Germany – 90 square metres – this could add another 22,000 apartments to the mix. Using a Bauhaus dwelling standard of 45 square metres would double that number.[19]

In the context of Germany's national housing shortage, one should pay special attention to the housing stock of the former East Germany, or rather, to the methodical elimination thereof. Since 1990, around 300,000 apartments have been demolished in the former German Democratic Republic – roughly the same number as the difference (318,000 units) between what Scholz promised and what was actually built.[20]

The Netherlands serves as another example. The country's housing shortfall is identified as being around 400,000 homes.[21] In 2022, the Dutch government, through a dedicated Minister of Housing and Spatial Planning, made an agreement with the provinces that 900,000 new homes would be built by 2030.[22] 90,000 were built in 2022 and 88,000 in 2023. That leaves 722,000 to go in six years, or around 120,000 per year.[23]

Meanwhile, European environmental rules have imposed strict limits on new construction projects. An impossible choice presents itself: the environment or the people. The discussion feels somewhat surreal given the fact that the population of the Netherlands has been stable for the last two decades. Most of its housing stock was built after 1970 and is in good condition. Why would they need more?

As the political sphere scrambles to find a compromise, the country polarizes. No resolution is in sight, only the successful prevention of an accurate assessment of the real situation. Since the last Dutch Planning Policy Note (Nota Ruimtelijke Ordening) from 2001, no proper inventory of the Netherlands' housing stock has been made, so there is no clarity on the relation between the amount of space needed and what already exists. How much habitable built space (including vacant office space) exists in the Netherlands per capita? A rough calculation dividing the estimated amount of habitable built space (including vacant office space) by the current population adds up to about 75 square metres – roughly 1.5 times the metreage that the early modernists defined as the 'Existenzminimum'.

In 2003, the debate took a bizarre turn when the Housing and Planning minister suggested that between 80,000 and 260,000 extra homes could be created in existing houses, apartments and vacant buildings by adding an extra floor or splitting a house into separate floors.[24]

Germany and the Netherlands are not alone. In Europe, there are several other countries where ambitious housing programmes are offset by massive vacancy rates. Ireland claims it needs to build 35,000 homes annually to keep up with population growth,[25] yet 160,000 properties are currently unoccupied, 48,000 of which have been built since 2016.[26] Portugal plans to construct 45,000 homes each year,[27] while 700,000 homes sit empty.[28] Belgium requires 225,000 new homes while 600,000 remain unoccupied across the country.[29] Switzerland needs 51,000 homes,[30] yet more than 54,000 remain vacant.[31] France has pledged to build 500,000 new homes,[32] even though 3.1 million properties are still empty.[33] Spain requires 600,000 homes,[34] but faces 3.8 million vacant properties.[35] Greece has a shortage of 210,000 homes,[36] contrasted with 700,000 vacancies.[37] Italy builds 60,000 homes yearly,[38] yet 10 million homes – one in every three – remain unoccupied.[39]

Shortages and vacancies . . . Hardly ever is a connection made between the two. Either vacant properties are not considered part of the solution because they are not for sale (often because it pays for owners to keep them empty), or they are dismissed as the wrong type of housing in the wrong place by policymakers or developers (often a combination of the two). Vacancies are thought to represent two ends of the spectrum with no relevance to mainstream requirements.

The arguments seem flimsy. Empty homes that are not for sale can either be subject to heavy taxation (as is happening in certain places) or to laws banning the phenomenon altogether. The second argument – wrong homes in the wrong place – is unconvincing given that it is commonly made by the same people who cite desperate housing shortages. Furthermore, given the increasingly footloose nature of work, 'the wrong place' qualifies as a bit of a misnomer.

The planning and building of large new urban developments while significant portions of the existing built environment remain empty goes against all common sense. Much is said about sustainability and forms of sustainable building. Well-intended as the notion may be, the uncomfortable reality is that how we approach things is simply *not* sustainable in its current form.

Our unrelenting urge to 'build away' our shortages comes with massive environmental consequences. The toll of the construction industry on the environment is well known, accounting for 50 per cent of global resource extraction,[40] 52 per cent of all steel[41] and 25 per cent of all aluminium[42] produced worldwide, and 16 per cent of the world's freshwater consumption.[43] Buildings produce 33 per cent of greenhouse gas emissions, are responsible for a third of of global energy use, and consume three quarters of all electricity produced,[44] while their demolition accounts for a third of all global waste. Furthermore, 30 per cent of particulate matter (PM10) emissions come from construction,[45] while 56 per cent of the occupational cancers in men are within the construction industry.[46] It is hardly possible to overstate the impact of construction on the global ecosystem.

Back to the question posed at the beginning of this chapter: do we need new buildings? The assumption that building more homes automatically leads to more affordable homes is increasingly being proven false. Rising house prices are not the result of scarcity. In Western Europe, where the housing crisis is high on the political agenda, most countries have had stable populations and housing stocks for more than twenty years. In countries where the population has grown, the housing stock has grown proportionally, and in some cases even outstripped population growth. In the UK, the massive increase in housing costs has even coincided with a growth in the amount of surplus housing. The UK also belies the explanation that the rise in housing costs is the result of reduced social housing stock: despite the mass sell-off of council housing since the 1980s, the percentage of socially rented dwellings is still nearly double the EU average.[47]

Rising house prices in the UK are not the result of undersupply, but of policies that have actively encouraged prices to rise. Until the 1980s, private rents in the UK had been capped and regulated by law. Thatcher's government changed all that. To attract capital, the rental market was deregulated, causing rents to rise and boost property values as a whole. In 2023, the real estate sector accounted for more than 13 per cent of the UK's total gross value added (GVA), two-thirds of that coming from housing.[48] Housing-based wealth is meanwhile central to the UK economy, described by some as the country's closest thing to a national industry.[49]

The trend has come to apply in most European countries. Real estate is the prime business of virtually every major city in Europe. In the race between value and price, the population is both the greatest beneficiary and the greatest victim. The rise in value of one property is annulled by an even sharper rise in price of the next. And that is for those lucky enough to own property. The 'richer' the city, the smaller the living space those on a median income can afford, if they can afford to live there at all . . .

Building more homes in the hope of driving down prices is proving a logic in reverse. We are building more than ever, and yet more homes do not lead to more affordable homes. It is time to recognize that we face not a housing crisis but an affordability crisis. Mistaking one for the other consistently forces us into a vicious cycle: to tackle the crisis, we build new homes; these too prove unaffordable, leading us to build yet more in turn.

More than a means to provide shelter, construction serves as a lucrative means of investment. It would be naive to expect the private parties who make their money from building our homes to go against their own interests by reducing prices. But does the same need to apply to architects? Too often architecture serves as a fig leaf for financial returns. Don't be fooled: speculative developers do not hire architects because they are so fond of their work, but because their involvement helps them secure the necessary approvals for large development quantums. Who could argue with culture?

No longer should architects allow their work to be abused in this way. Let's refuse to play ball and see what happens; abstain from planning and designing new buildings until the conditions have fundamentally changed. There are plenty of alternatives. The days when projects started from a tabula rasa are long gone. Few proposed building sites have no existing buildings, or existing structures of some sort. We could start by opposing their demolition and spending our creative energies inventing new ways in which existing environments could have a second (third, fourth or fifth) lease of life. Let's not waste our time on new buildings until we run out of existing ones. The present wave of construction has nothing to do with housing the masses. Stop building, and the dirty secret will expose itself.

11

What's Done Is Done

It weighed over 5 tonnes. And it had been a gargantuan effort to get it up there, lifted by a crane onto six fixtures, counterbalanced by three water tanks holding 1,000 litres each. Preparations had taken more than two years. A miniature made of clay had preceded a life-size plaster model. After that, the welders had taken over, constructing a stainless-steel skeleton to support 1-millimetre-thick sheets of copper, patinated against verdigris and polished with wax. Eight by eight metres it measured: the 'great seal' carrying the Prussian coat of arms, framed by fluttering griffins and soldered palm, complete with sceptre, orb and a medal chain with black eagles, graced by a metre-high crown covered with 300 grams of gold leaf at the top and a Prussian order star retrieved from the museum depot dangling from the bottom.

Endlich ist es soweit! Ten years after the laying of the foundational stone in 2013, the installation of the great seal is the final act in the reconstruction (or rather rebuilding) of the

Berlin Palace, or Stadtschloss Berlin. Apart from the order star, there is nothing real or original about the decorative item. Just as there is nothing real or original about the building to which it is attached – a reincarnation of a building from bygone days, the suitability of which has divided opinion in Berlin for over two decades and continues to do so even after its completion. Essential to restoring the integrity and cohesion of Berlin's historic centre to some, to others the Stadtschloss Berlin was an inappropriate reminder of Germany's imperial past.

Residence of the Hohenzollern, epicentre of the Prussian Revolution, symbolic heart of the German Empire, launching pad of the German Socialist Republic, made into a museum during the Weimar Republic, ignored by the Nazis, bombed by the Allies, its ruin a backdrop to a Soviet war movie... More than a testament to Germany's imperial past, the old Berliner Schloss is a testament to all of Germany's histories combined. In retrospect, the building was a marvel of adaptability and reuse. That is, until the division of Germany abruptly put an end to things and razed it to the ground.

Reconstruction of the Schloss had been planned since the fall of the Berlin Wall, with endless arguments being exchanged for and against: objections to the exorbitant cost were met with claims about the long-term economic benefits to the city; a predicted lack of skilled workers with an optimistic portrayal of the project as an employment programme; the alleged absence of detailed drawings with evidence that a rebuilding could just as easily be done from photographic documentation; and suggestions of 'Disneyfication' with the simple truth that, to some extent, all existing historical buildings, by dint of ageing and repair, are at least partial reconstructions.

In the end, the advocates of the reconstruction won. They argued that historical buildings possess not only a material value but also an immaterial significance – as recognized by UNESCO's principles – and the latter justifies reconstruction when it acts to preserve urban and historical identity, provided sufficient documentation for an 'authentic copy' exists, of course. The rebuilt Schloss, they claimed, would restore coherence to Berlin's city centre and become a magnet for visitors not only in Germany but in all of central Europe.[1]

And indeed, in 2007, even if somewhat in the form of a compromise, the German Bundestag decided to press ahead with the reconstruction plans: three of the Schloss facades were to be replicas of the original, while the fourth was to reflect the more contemporary aspirations of its new occupant: the newly established Humboldt Forum. The museum finally opened its doors to the public in 2021 (after digitally opening in 2020), going down as the most expensive cultural project in German history.

We have torn down more buildings during the past twenty-five years than in all of the previous century. Old buildings must make way for new, bigger, better and 'smarter' ones as a matter of routine. A halt to new construction would inevitably change that logic. If we stop building, we are going to need every building we can get our hands on. No longer can we afford to dismiss buildings as non-compliant with contemporary standards – be they technical, financial or ideological. Replacing any building with a supposedly more sustainable one is in itself an unsustainable act – as is the demolition of buildings simply because they are incompatible with prevailing political views.

History moves in mysterious ways. In the case of the Berliner Schloss, the supreme irony is that the key argument *in favour* of reconstruction – the invocation of an evolving UNESCO stance – could just as much have been leveraged *against* it. As of 1972, UNESCO deemed full-scale rebuilding acceptable when historic structures had disappeared as a result of conflict or disaster. The Schloss had disappeared because of changing political winds. Insofar as these qualify as disaster, the same UNESCO position that brought back the Schloss could have been invoked to preserve the building that was demolished to make way for it: the Palast der Republik, the modernist bronze-mirrored glass palace that had hosted the parliament, or Volkskammer, of the now-extinct German Democratic Republic.

The Palast too had a public function; the Palast too hosted a museum; the Palast too represented the immaterial significance of an age; the Palast too was an integral part of German history, and, just like the Schloss in 1950, the Palast could have been saved. The asbestos that contaminated its interior had mostly been boxed in, and where it wasn't it could have been removed. The presence of asbestos was no more a valid reason for the demolition of the Palast than the damage inflicted by allied bombings had been for the Schloss. Just like the demolition of the Schloss in 1950, the demolition of the Palast was a product of political motivation, not of pragmatic, functional or even historical considerations.

The Palast was Honecker's gift to the people – the collective reward for a society devoted to collective ideals. An opulent manifestation of everything the GDR had to offer, located prominently in the middle of the city, along Unter den Linden, giving new symbolic meaning to a site once befouled by a symbol of Prussian Imperialism. Constructed in the mid-seventies (within a mere three years), the Palast delivered physical proof that the communist world was now fully on par with the west, in terms of both technical competence and demonstrable wealth. Lavish marble walls, sumptuously polished floors and glittering light features – all of a bridal whiteness.

The purpose of the building, housing the Volkskammer, was a sidenote. With the exception of the parliamentary hall, most of the building's functions were public. It contained two large auditoria, art galleries, a theatre, a cinema, thirteen restaurants, five beer halls, a bowling alley, billiard rooms, a rooftop ice skating ring, a private gym with spa, a casino, a medical station, a post office, a police station with an underground cellblock, an indoor basketball court, an indoor swimming pool, a private barbershop and salons, public and private restrooms and a discothèque – all open for extensive hours of the day. In today's terminology, the Palast qualified as an unequivocal example of placemaking: East Berlin's living room.[2]

The Palast der Republik was eventually demolished in 2006. An ambitious plan for a makeover as Berlin's equivalent of the Pompidou Centre failed to make the cut. Various improvised uses like the Terracotta Army exhibition or a concert by Einstürzende Neubauten may have somewhat prolonged the Palast's life, but in the end could not prevent its disappearance. A mere thirty years after its completion, the Palace of the People was no more, razed to make way for a building that had been razed half a century earlier. No city tests the linear logic in time like Berlin.

A 2004 documentary broadcast on Dutch TV about the imminent demolition of the Palast features various actors in the building's life.[3] All are roughly the same age: the architect, the caretaker, a former East German art historian and the cleaning lady. The opposing yet similar accounts given by the latter two are compelling. The art historian recalls how the Schloss exhibited impressionist paintings brought in from the Louvre by the allied occupiers, paintings she had never been able to admire before. Fond are her memories of the Schloss, and equally bitter her memories of how Ulbricht and his clique brutally put an end to it all. Recounting the wrecking ball's first punch moves her to tears. Five minutes on, the cleaning lady is similarly overcome with emotion. She too is vexed in her pride. And, just like the historian, her anguish is caused by wrecking balls, only this time it is the ones ripping into the Palast.

Demolition did not mean the end of the Palast's physical substance. Like an organ donor lives on in the body of the recipient, the Palast der Republik gets to live on in the DNA of a new building. In 2008, its 35,000 tonnes of steel were shipped to the United Arab Emirates, to be recycled into the structure of Burj Khalifa – another iconic building designed at the whim of the powers that be. Not unsuccessfully. In its relatively short existence Burj has already withstood one major instance of political turmoil, and it did so not by undergoing any significant reconstruction, but merely by a change of name.

Not so the Palast. Inevitably, its fate was tied to that of the Republik, which, like the Palast, no longer exists. Just like the system of which it was a part, and that had once spanned half the globe. Not counting Cuba, the GDR was the westernmost outpost of the communist world – a billboard facing towards an incredulous west. In the forty years of its existence, the country embarked on a construction programme unparalleled in history – a radical response to a desperate shortage of housing after the Second World War – only to be met by an equally relentless demolition effort following its dissolution.

New arrivals have come on the scene meanwhile. And while the numbers indicate that the GDR's one-time housing stock could have easily met the associated need, those new arrivals must instead be housed in containers or other makeshift homes. In a bizarre plot twist, temporary homes take the place of hastily demolished permanent ones. A national controversy arises from a missed opportunity.

The built legacy of the GDR is like text within parentheses: whatever is written in between can be removed without altering the course of the narrative. But how much of recent history can legitimately be viewed as expendable subtext?

The heyday of the GDR's construction programme, the 1960s and '70s, coincided with similar, and similarly radical, efforts in the West. And, like in the GDR, the results have since attracted similar disproval. The Conservative Party in the UK has tried to politicize the discussion on architecture in the context of (a lack of) beauty, demonizing much of its postwar past. In the Netherlands, populist politicians have made modern architecture fair game in the context of a broader attack on progressive values.

The trend is not limited to politicians. Architects too, are waging war on the work of their modernist predecessors. In his latest book *Humanize*, Thomas Heatherwick implies a causal relation between the (belated) influence of modernists such as Le Corbusier and Mies and the cold and alienating nature of the current built environment. In the Netherlands,

Sjoerd Soeters equates the legacy of the Bauhaus to boredom. The winner of the 2023 RIBA Gold Medal, Yasmeen Lari, has gone as far as to offer a public apology for her own former Brutalist work.

The relentless portrayal of 1960s and '70s architecture as alienating and inhumane is becoming a self-fulfilling prophecy. There is no other historical period whose buildings are being demolished or threatened with demolition in the same way.

How wise is any of this? The environmental impact, for one, is catastrophic. The ecological consequences of the effort to put new buildings in place, in terms of resource extraction, energy use and greenhouse gas emissions, are well known.[4] On average, the decision to refurbish rather than demolish and rebuild represents a 30 per cent reduction in CO_2 emissions. Equally disconcerting are the financial consequences. The excessive costs of rebuilding the Berliner Schloss have been well documented, but in less extravagant cases the refurbishment of existing buildings also proves to be the cheaper option, representing a 20–30 and sometimes 50 per cent reduction in cost. Lacaton & Vassal's renovation of the 1960s Tour Bois-le-Prêtre in Paris, previously nicknamed Alcatraz, cost €65,000 per apartment, about a third of the estimated cost to demolish and rebuild.[5] Same with the Cité du Grand Parc in Bordeaux, also built in the 1960s, and refurbished by Lacaton & Vassal at €50,000 per unit.[6] The Kleiburg in Amsterdam – one of the few apartment buildings from the 1970s Bijlmermeer neighbourhood, once notorious for its high crime rates, to escape demolition – was renovated at a cost low enough to allow its apartments to be sold for just €1,200 per square metre, cheaper than any newly built units in the city.[7] In the UK, the renovation of Park Hill Estate in Sheffield by developer Urban Splash also made real estate developers realize the financial advantages of retrofitting over demolition and new construction, albeit targeting more affluent residents.

Such numbers are by no means limited to residential projects. At present, the Glenbow museum in Calgary faces structural repairs, modernization of interiors and various energy efficiency upgrades. The associated cost of $450 per square foot compares to $1,000–$1,100 per square foot for a new build. In terms of environmental impact, the refurbishment avoided 56,000 tonnes of new carbon being produced over the lifespan of the building, because operational carbon has been greatly reduced, and kept 38,000 tonnes of concrete out of landfill.[8]

The NT Future refurbishment project at the National Theatre in London, completed in 2015, cost approximately £80 million. This included upgrades to the building's mechanical and electrical systems, insulation improvements and interior refurbishments to better accommodate modern audiences. These efforts are expected to reduce the operational carbon emissions of the National Theatre by around 30 per cent.[9] The estimated cost to demolish it and rebuild a facility of similar size and functionality ranged between £140 and £300 million.[10]

The cost savings associated with refurbishment are mostly common knowledge. However, that doesn't automatically tip the balance in its favour. Far from it. As long as the revenue from buildings, in the form of either rents or value appreciation, continues to outstrip the cost of making them, the demolition of existing buildings remains an attractive financial proposition. The opportunity cost of ever larger, ever more profitable buildings on any given piece of land sustains a perpetual and very profitable cycle of new buildings. The resulting paradox is both understandable and dispiriting. While the built volume of our cities is forever on the increase, its availability to the average earner surely isn't.

Nowhere is this more visible than in the domain of housing, where demolition continues to be the preferred option. Although most countries tend to be guarded about the exact numbers, the juxtaposition made in Chapter 10, showing the bizarre contrast between ambitious housing programmes and present vacancy rates, can similarly be made in relation to demolitions of the social housing stock in various countries.

France has pledged to build 500,000 new homes,[11] even though 50,000 are demolished annually.[12] The housing shortage in the Netherlands is estimated at 400,000,[13] while nearly 100,000 homes have been torn down over the last decade.[14] Italy builds 60,000 homes yearly, but also demolishes 8,000 every year.[15] England requires 300,000 new homes per year,[16] even though 50,000 homes are demolished each year.[17] The situation is particularly bad in Scotland, which plans to construct 35,000 social houses by 2026;[18] at the same time it has demolished more than 77,000 homes.[19] Ireland claims it needs to build 35,000 homes annually to keep up with population growth,[20] yet 40,000 properties have been demolished in the last decade.[21] And the situation isn't limited to Europe. The United States faces a shortfall of 7.2 million homes[22] despite 300,000 homes being demolished annually.[23]

Extensive demolitions are often justified in terms of buildings' non-compliance with current technical or environmental standards. Such arguments particularly target housing from the 1960s and '70s. And yet the evolution of building technology has been stagnant for at least 100 years. The structural systems applied to new buildings are not significantly different to those of fifty years ago. Moreover, when it comes to environmental standards – or more precisely 'building physics' – both the cost and the environmental footprint of conversion would still be much lower than building new. One wonders, is it the buildings that are out of place or the political ideology that begat them?

Saving the planet, or saving the construction industry? If the world were indeed to follow through with a moratorium on new buildings as stipulated in the previous chapter, we would rapidly approach the point where demolition becomes taboo. We would need every building there is. Certainly, we can no longer afford to evaluate buildings based on the political ideology that brought them into being, or even on the function for which they were originally designed.

On this score, the COVID-19 pandemic revealed an interesting truth. Hastily assembled army tents served as triage facilities; the sports centre in Wuhan was turned into a temporary hospital early on, followed by the Pacaembu Stadium in São Paulo and the CFR stadium in Timişoara; the IFEMA expo centres in Madrid and the Jacob K. Javits Convention Center in New York doubled as hospitals, as did the Belgrade Fair, the Excel Centre in London and the Fiera Milano.

But beyond conversions into hospitals alone, the lifespan of existing buildings offers ample evidence of their changeability, full stop. (Almost) every building can assume the function of (almost) every other building. Residential buildings aside, there are precious few buildings over fifty years old that have retained their original purpose.

A few examples: the James A. Farley Building in Midtown Manhattan was converted from a post office to a train hall. The Mid-Manhattan Library is housed in the former Arnold Constable & Company department store. The empty Euclid Square Mall in Euclid, Ohio, is under reconstruction to become the home of a new Amazon fulfilment centre. The Pionen nuclear bunker in Stockholm has been converted into a data centre, while the dilapidated German war bunker at Vuren, in the Netherlands, has been transformed into a temporary holiday retreat. The 100-year-old church in Llanera, Spain has been transformed into a skatepark, while the Jopen church in Haarlem, the Netherlands has been converted into a brewery. The fire station in Avignon is now a theatre school. The world's largest startup campus in Paris is housed in a former tram depot. In the same city, the former Orsay railway station has been converted into a museum, as has the Hamburger Bahnhof in Berlin. The former airport Tempelhof in Berlin has been converted into an office park, and the TWA terminal at JFK is now a hotel. The former Charles Street Jail in Boston serves as a luxury hotel, while the former Bijlmer prison in Amsterdam now houses refugees. Madrid's Matadero art centre used to be a slaughterhouse. The former locomotive factory in Tilburg, the Netherlands has been converted into a library. In Brandenburg, Germany, a former airship hangar has been converted into a tropical garden, while the one in Riga has been converted into a market. The Arcola Theatre in London is housed in the former Colourworks paint factory. The Biblioteca de México José Vasconcelos is housed in a former tobacco factory. A former tobacco factory also houses the Hellenic Parliament Library & Printing House. A former filling station at London's King's Cross currently houses a cultural centre. The New Jersey Bell Labs research centre now serves as a mixed-use office for high-tech startup companies. Victoria Baths, a former swimming pool in Manchester, currently functions as an event space. Both the parliament of Andalusia and the Library of Catalonia in Barcelona are located in former hospitals, while Milan's former Hospitale Maggiore has come to serve as a university.

If buildings are readily changeable, even more so are the opinions about them. At the time of its inception, the Eiffel Tower was perceived as a slight against French taste by writers, painters, sculptors, architects and other passionate devotees of the hitherto untouched beauty of Paris – 'a gigantic factory chimney, crushing under its barbaric weight Notre Dame, the Sainte-Chapelle, the Dome of Les Invalides, the Arc de Triomphe, all of our humiliated monuments'.[24] The Cathedral of Christ the Savior in Moscow served as one of the most significant examples of Russian architecture until the twentieth century. It was then demolished under communist rule in 1931, only to be rebuilt in the 1990s. Brutalist architecture, the physical manifestation of the postwar welfare state, became the discarded symbol of its undoing, only to become a cultural fetish after the MoMA exhibition of 2018.

Just as opinions about the built environment are ever changing, so are policies aimed at its preservation. The link between preservation and periods of destruction or war is unmistakable. We cling on most to what we fear will be imminently lost. In France, the first initiatives to protect the nation's heritage came following the vandalism of the French Revolution. In the UK, preservation was triggered by the destruction wrought by the Industrial Revolution, and by railway construction in particular. In 1945, following the devastations of the Second World War, UNESCO was set up as a specialized agency of the United Nations 'to build peace through international cooperation in Education, the Sciences and Culture'.

Its view was formalized as follows: 'When, as the result of decay or destruction, restoration appears to be indispensable, [UNESCO] recommends that the historic and artistic work of the past should be respected, without excluding the style of any given period.'[25] The extent to which new functions are expected to serve or threaten what is being preserved remains ambiguous: 'the occupation of buildings, which ensures the continuity of their life, should be maintained but . . . they should be used for a purpose which respects their historic or artistic character'.

The later Venice Charter of 1964 replicates the same ambiguity: 'The conservation of monuments is always facilitated by making use of them for some socially useful purpose. Such use is therefore desirable but it must not change the lay-out or decoration of the building. It is within these limits only that modifications demanded by a change of function should be envisaged and may be permitted.'[26]

A stop on new buildings logically entails an end to demolitions. In terms of preservation, that could mark an interesting paradigm shift. Preservation policies are inevitably based on a choice between what is worth preserving and what is not. They are moral by definition. Moreover, in dictating which projected uses are deemed acceptable, their moral verdict on the past gets to extend into the future. A moratorium on *new* construction will inevitably force the wholesale mobilization of the past. That mobilization will render all moral verdicts obsolete. No longer will the aim of preserving buildings set a condition for their use; instead, the unconditional use of every building comes to equal the unconditional preservation of all. A building halt will make preservation at once all-important and not important at all.

Pardon all things built and finally we will be able to see buildings for what they are: the silent witnesses of history, an inextricable mix of (and beyond) good and evil, just like history itself. Abstinence from building in the present would simply serve to underline the importance of all other periods combined, no matter what. Cancel culture has no place. The self-promotion of current architects at the expense of their predecessors is a no-go. Heatherwick and Co will have to find new employment as home converters, perhaps starting with a few modernist villas slated for demolition. All fruitless discussions on the perceived architectural crimes of previous epochs stop here, as do all biased preservation policies, if only because from here on preservation is the default mode.

No longer will history have to be treated with the perfunctory respect that is commonly expected of us. Once again, it can become the subject of creation, not mere 'context' – to be ignored at will – but matter to work with. A renewed focus on the existing could undo a whole series of tiresome oppositions which, in one way or another, are holding our discipline hostage: between past and present, problem and solution, observing and acting, analysis and intervention. In architecture schools, the history of architecture could become an applied science and architectural design an art of quiet contemplation. The real revolution in our profession may not reside in things to come but in what is already here. We can rest at ease, busier than ever.

12

Unlearn Vitruvius

He was trained by Mies van der Rohe, as one of the last generation of students at the Bauhaus and later as an employee of Mies's Chicago office. That was also where he must have inherited his master's most defining trait: the monomaniac striving for perfection, doing the same thing over and over again, slightly better each time. Yet, where Mies's efforts were directed at archetypes, virtually independent of function, Bertrand Goldberg was a functionalist in the extreme, whose work included highly bespoke housing projects, offices, commercial buildings and banks.

Perfection and functionality tend to be a tricky combination. Catering to both inevitably narrows the scope of their combined plausibility. It led Goldberg to devote the better part of his career to the perfection of a single building typology: the hospital.

It took him a while to get there. His first four hospital projects – all designed during the early 1960s – remained unbuilt. It hardly mattered to the architect: 'creation is a patient search'.[1] These projects were only dress rehearsals for the real thing, as were the two first hospitals Goldberg actually built – the Elgin State Hospital in Elgin, Illinois, completed in 1967, and St Joseph Hospital in Tacoma, Washington, in 1974.

Goldberg's 'perfect' creation eventually saw the light of day in 1975: the Prentice Women's Hospital in Chicago. Prentice was to be the hospital to end all hospitals – or at least the need to design any other type of hospital in the future. After Prentice, all any prospective hospital builder needed to do was acquire the blueprints of its construction drawings, find a contractor and break ground. From here, Goldberg's architect-colleagues would be free to spend their creative energy on other building typologies.

Goldberg continued to practise until his death in 1997 – long enough to see time get the better of his perfect conception, but, luckily for him, not so long as to have to witness its ultimate fate. At the time of his passing, Prentice was already facing serious challenges in meeting the ever-evolving requirements of healthcare. In 2007, those challenges had become such that the operator decided to build a new facility. Prentice was subsequently vacated in 2011 and demolished in 2014, despite protests from local residents, architects – including six Pritzker Prize winners – and a proposal to build a thirty-one-story tower on top of it. The operator justified the decision as follows: 'The current structure is not useable for medical research. There are problems with the floor plans and the ceiling height does not meet the required standards. And there simply isn't enough space. We intend to build a larger building on that site for twenty-first-century medical research.'[2]

A mere thirty-nine years after its opening, the hospital to end all hospitals was no more. The biomedical research facility that stands in its place is meanwhile due for its fifth conversion. In the race towards innovation, architecture is no match for medical science.

'When we build, let us think that we build for ever', wrote John Ruskin in 1849.[3] Ruskin's words are exemplary: the myth of building for eternity has pervaded the mindset of architects for as long as they have existed. Most buildings do not live up to the expectation. In fact, the majority of buildings erected in history have disappeared. We dedicate our creative lives to the creation of buildings. Almost never do we think of their disappearance, let alone devote our creativity to it. The consequences of that neglect are huge: when buildings eventually do have to go, their demolition comes with massive environmental consequences; supposedly permanent typologies are in a permanent state of conversion, compromising both their functionality and experiential quality; and the adaptability of buildings vis-à-vis the effects of climate change is an afterthought at best.

An analysis of the lifespan of buildings throughout history reveals an interesting paradox: the more recent their construction, the sooner they appear to be ready for the wrecking ball. If we are to extrapolate this trend into the future, buildings may soon be obsolete on, or even before, completion. No longer can we afford to design buildings without thinking of their removal in tandem. There simply isn't the time.

The following list may serve as proof of the trend: the Palais des Tuileries in Paris (1564) was demolished after 319 years; Les Halles (1870) after 100 years. Penn Station, New York

(1910) was replaced by a new version after fifty-three years. The Miami Herald building (1963), the newspaper's headquarters, was demolished in 2015 after fifty-two years. The Tricorn Centre shopping complex in Portsmouth (1966) was demolished in 2004 after thirty-eight years. The Pagoda tower in Madrid (1968), headquarters of the Jorba Pharmaceutical company, was demolished in 1999 after thirty-one years. The Omni Coliseum in Atlanta (1972) was demolished in 1997 after twenty-five years. The 69,000-seat Stadio delle Alpi in Turin (1990), built for the World Cup in 1990 and home to local football clubs Juventus Torino and AC Torino, was demolished in 2009 after nineteen years. The American Folk Art Museum in New York (2001), by Tod Williams Billie Tsien Architects, was demolished in 2014 after thirteen years – probably a world record.

Even when buildings are not slated for demolition, they are barely a credible testament to permanence. Following flooding in 2008, Farnsworth House had to crowdfund the restoration of its terrace. In 2011, the Eames Foundation launched the 250-Year Project to 'make sure that when your great, great, great, great grandchildren visit the Eames House in the future, they will be able to have the same authentic experience that you can have today'.[4] In 2023, the Sydney Opera House reopened after a decade of renovation at a cost of A$150 million. In 2015, the UN Headquarters celebrated its seventy-year anniversary with the conclusion of a fifteen-year renovation that cost $2.3 billion. Fifty years after its completion, Montparnasse Tower is in drastic need of renovation, and many Parisians, in fact, would prefer the building gone. In 2025, forty-seven years after it first opened, the Pompidou Centre closed its doors to the public for 'a major revamp' estimated to cost €358 million. The renovation of 'New York's most energetically wasteful office building', the Seagram Building, is long overdue and meeting with increasing scepticism as to whether it is even worth it.[5]

'All buildings must be built with due reference to durability, convenience, and beauty.'[6] While Vitruvius, and many since, have theorized about the durability and eternal destiny of buildings, it is interesting to note that Roman construction practice itself was in reality considerably less enduring. Frequently, in the construction of new monuments or buildings, the concept of *spoliatum*, or 'robbing', was applied. Existing monuments, particularly those of conquered cities, were dismantled and parts of them brought back to Rome to be recycled in new projects. Marble and granite were often drawn from buildings instead of quarries. Existing structures became the raw material for new ones.

Spoliatum was not exclusive to the Empire's new territories. In Rome itself, monuments erected by former rulers were used to build new ones. The Arch of Constantine incorporates friezes and reliefs from monuments originally dedicated by Trajan, Hadrian and Marcus Aurelius. The Arch of Janus, dating also from Emperor Constantine's time, was built with marble blocks from the Temple of Venus and Roma, some 2 kilometres away. Later, in the ninth century, the arch itself was a material source for the nearby church of San Giorgio in Velabro. In the following centuries, many churches were erected using materials from former temples.

The recycling of building elements was a well-developed and flourishing industry in the Roman Empire, involving a series of complex operations typical of a production cycle, ranging from the recovery of the material through to its transportation and re-assembly in a completely new architectural style. Whereas in the Arch of Constantine the blocks of *spolia* are clearly visible and serve as a sign of prestige, in the Arch of Janus the reused material was completely reshaped to conceal its origin.

The recycling of materials also involved more trivial elements. Amphorae and sarcophagi were frequently reused. So were bricks, tiles, marble tiles and stone blocks. At other times their function changed: slabs of reliefs were used as sarcophagi, while sarcophagi were used as latrine seats. Objects and construction elements were often broken up to create new materials. Fragmented amphorae were used either as a floor underlayer, pigment or, mixed with lime, as a waterproof coating. Marble was burned to produce lime of the best quality.

The practice involved precise activities, starting with the identification and cataloguing of the elements, and making sure they could be extracted in a way that would not cause the total collapse of the structures. Their processing took place in specialized workshops. One such workshop was discovered in the suburbs of Rome in the bath complex of a villa that was itself repurposed, which made perfect sense: Roman villas were built along important commercial routes and consisted of different pavilions where each stage of the processing cycle could take place independently. For instance, burning the marble was done in the room formerly used for hot baths, while the cooling of the resulting lime took place in the pool of the former cold baths.

Roman practice is not the only one to signify a gap between theory and praxis. Many architectural marvels we treasure in the name of authenticity have a much more tampered-with history than we think. It is not rare for 'originals' to be a carefully staged illusion. Much of Renaissance Venice is a nineteenth-century reconstruction; the Venice Campanile dates from 1910 and Teatro La Fenice from 2003. The Vienna Opera and Milan's La Scala date from the late 1940s. All the sections of the Eiffel Tower have been replaced at least once. The Lincoln Bedroom dates from the Truman administration.

This phenomenon is not limited to the nineteenth and twentieth centuries. The *Blue Guide* to London tells us that Inigo Jones's Banqueting House was completed in 1622, but does not inform us that what we are seeing is John Soane's refacing of 1829. Soane's work was itself not exempt: his Dulwich Picture Gallery is a 1950s reconstruction of the original, destroyed in the war.

Just as architecture is equated with permanence, permanence itself is equated with mass and solidity. This staunch preconception has withstood even the harshest reality checks of construction practices over time. And yet, much of architecture history hints at an evolution in the opposite direction. One of the hallmark innovations of the Renaissance was the extensive use of arches, vaults and domes, which allowed a more even distribution of weight and thus larger, open interior spaces with fewer and less massive supporting walls. (Brunelleschi's dome for Florence Cathedral is an example of structural ingenuity.) The introduction of pointed arches, ribbed vaults and flying buttresses in the Gothic cathedral allowed soaring, airy structures with thinner walls and larger windows. The economy of materials came to be equated to beauty, to doing more with less. Where the construction of the Gothic cathedral was largely a matter of custom, with a gradual perfecting of known techniques, the introduction of industrial technologies in the nineteenth century took things to another level. An unprecedented reduction in weight allowed the Crystal Palace to remain completely free of heavy masonry for supporting walls or foundations.

The widespread use of mass-produced steel (and by default reinforced concrete) in the twentieth century changed the way we build forever. Structure, once the defining feature of architectural expression, became a minority component of buildings. In the Parthenon, 50 per cent of the built volume was consumed by structure. To compare, in Le Corbusier's 1914 Maison Domino, structure consumed less than 5 per cent of the building volume. The associated *plan libre* marked the rigorous separation between structure and non-structure and marked the 'liberation', i.e. free treatment, of the latter, in the same way as fixtures or furniture, literally sometimes, as in the case of the curtain wall.

Although scarcely evidenced in Le Corbusier's own buildings, the *plan libre* also signalled another important evolution, namely the liberation of substantial parts of a building from the primitivity of construction sites. Not only could the non-structural parts be 'freely' designed, they could also be freely produced 'off-site', allowed to enter the realm of manufacturing and thereby reach a level of technical sophistication impossible to achieve on a building site.

The design of lightweight, industrially produced buildings became a central pursuit of the twentieth-century architecture avant-garde. The components of Jean Prouvé's prototypical houses were designed to be flat and lightweight so they could be transported on a cargo plane. Of his House Coque, a construction system designed to house workers at a Citroën factory, Prouvé said: 'I am ready to mass-produce manufactured houses, as Citroën did in 1919 for automobiles.'[7] In the 1940s, Konrad Wachsmann and Walter Gropius developed the Packaged House, a prefabricated modular construction system to house US troops and strategic equipment. In the 1940s and '50s, Case Study Houses in Los Angeles, designed by architects such as Charles and Ray Eames, Craig Ellwood and Eero Saarinen, served as inexpensive, industrially produced homes for returning soldiers. In Germany, the material economy of the Gothic cathedral found its culmination in the tensile structures of the German architect and engineer, Frei Otto.

Even more than in the efforts of Prouvé, the Eameses, Gropius, Wachsmann or Otto, the view of buildings as industrial products and the celebration of the associated efficiency gains finds its ultimate expression in the work of Richard Buckminster Fuller. Conceiving of the world as evolving towards a state of 'ephemeralization', Fuller was the construction industry's first real advocate of weightlessness, and was critical even of the mass-produced buildings of the time: 'The best of them weighs twenty times as much per useful interior cubic foot as does the useful cabin space of PAA's "China Clipper," despite the luxurious comfort of the Clipper's cabin, and the fact that it has climatic requirements far in excess of the house.'[8]

Insofar as Fuller represents a milestone in the inevitable evolution towards an ever more 'weightless' architecture, the continued adherence to Vitruvian principles exposes the architecture profession as deeply at odds with its historical destiny – stuck in the contradiction that while good construction requires a minimal use of materials, architecture itself is expected to convey an impression of permanence through solidity and mass.

That contradiction has been exacerbated by the increased emphasis on building performance in recent decades. Requirements in terms of fireproofing, thermal insulation and climate control mean that even the most manifest monolith is inevitably built as an assemblage of layers. Even the integrity of structure must give way to the logic of energy conservation. Rainscreens, suspended ceilings, raised floors, plasterboard walls, tiles disguised as heavy stones, razor-thin sheets of granite, marble or travertine to suggest the perfect two-dimensional mass.

The hollow sound you get from knocking on a supposedly solid piece of stone is the quintessential experience of any contemporary building. Even *béton brut* comes in the form of cladding. There is zero mass left in modern buildings. What you see is never what you get. Just as the human body is more than 90 per cent water, the contemporary building is more than 90 per cent air: the best insulator of all, guardian of the perfect climate.

Most architects frown on the realities of contemporary construction. Not least because facing up to these realities implies the abandonment of a professional ethos developed over centuries. The stubborn insistence on that ethos condemns every contemporary building to a form of stagecraft, enacting a play in denial of its own true nature. Most buildings are a cover-up, literally.

Even modern architecture is at odds with the practices of modern construction. Especially modern architecture, in fact. The earnest representation of structure, the absence of fluff, the celebration of the true nature of the materials applied . . . All hit a wall with the primacy of energy efficiency. Present-day buildings are all fluff. Inevitably so. Not space, but air is the real paradigm of contemporary architecture – just as (hot) air is the main currency of almost all contemporary architectural debate.

In the same way that the emphasis on solidity and mass in architecture serves to mask an evolution towards weightlessness, the insistence on durability similarly masks an evolution towards ever more instantaneous forms of construction. The Crystal Palace, three times the size of Saint Paul's Cathedral, was built in 190 days; Saint Paul's took thirty-five years. Kisho Kurokawa's five-story Takara Beautilion took a mere six days to put together, while Prouvé's BLPS steel-frame weekend house could be assembled by five workers in five hours. More recently, Wuhan demonstrated that the process of planning and building a hospital – a process normally taking ten years – could be reduced to a week.

Inexplicably, the increasingly instant nature of construction has barely affected the way we conceive of demolitions. The eventual disappearance of buildings is still very much a concern in terms of future generations, despite demolition proving an ever more pressing and imminent affair. The list of demolished buildings given at the outset of this chapter revealed that the more modern a building is – the more supposedly state-of-the-art – the sooner it proves to be out of date. Highly bespoke typologies like hospitals and laboratories receive their coup de grace from the all-consuming need for flexibility. In plain terms: before too long, we may have to start planning for the obsolescence of buildings even before their completion.

'A child can do it!' In a recent Bloomberg interview, Donald Trump complained about the lack of proper manufacturing jobs in the American automobile industry, describing US car plants as merely places for the assembly of foreign-made parts.[9] When it comes to construction sites, that might be something to rejoice over. The more buildings are put together as composites of prefabricated parts, the more readily they can also be taken apart. Currently, the construction industry generates around a third of global waste. Ninety per cent of that comes from demolitions and renovations. By far the largest net contributor is waste from the demolition of buildings that were expressly intended to be permanent. Waste is presumed to be an integral byproduct of building; more so it seems that (much of that) waste stems from a deeply misguided notion of building itself. We tend to equate sustainability with permanence. This may be one of the biggest mistakes of our time; sustainability might be better thought of as a responsible form of transience.

Sustainability has a twofold definition: 1) the quality of being able to continue over a long period of time; 2) the quality of causing little or no damage to the environment over a long period of time. It is important to note that the term was originally invented to optimize processes, *not* things. In that respect, it may be applicable to building, but it cannot apply in the same way to *a* building. In fact, the more we apply the term to buildings, the more we are caught in a vicious loop. Most buildings do not last – and the more they are built as if they do, the greater the damage they cause to the environment when they eventually don't. When it comes to buildings as things, definition 1 is inevitably, and fatally, set on a collision course with definition 2.

Only if buildings were truly eternal – their use infinitely changeable, their upgrades free of environmental cost, and the need to maintain them non-existent – might the two definitions meet in sync. In the real world those conditions do not exist. (Even the pyramids need routine maintenance.) The overall life of a building may be some fifty years, but the life of its mechanical systems is more likely to be limited to thirty. Certain facade systems don't last even twenty years. Single-ply roofing can typically be expected to last fifteen to twenty years, while the life of some types of caulking doesn't even exceed ten years. We tend to be scandalized by the idea, but it serves us well to realize that the doors of certain types of planes must be re-caulked before every flight.

'Permanence' only comes with permanent upkeep and adaptation. Yet these types of post-occupancy realities tend to be absent from the architect's radar. Here, the origin of the term sustainability – related to process, not things – once more comes into play. Only a conception of buildings as a process offers a realistic prospect of their adhering to the idea of sustainability. Machines to live in . . . if we persist with the analogy, we must be prepared to operate and maintain buildings like we do machines, and when that no longer suffices, eventually take them apart and recycle their spare parts.

Key to Roman construction practice was the fact that it didn't adhere to its own morals; that practice defied theory to become a theory of its own. Rome gave a particular twist to Vitruvius's professed ethos of *firmitas*, *utilitas* and *venustas* –

to the extent that it was not the ethos but the twist on it that sustained common practice.

Words are words; practice is practice. Any plausible relation between the two resides in the acknowledgement of the anything but subtle differences between them.

If we truly want to sustain the notion of building in future times, it is imperative that we apply an equally 'Roman twist' to the notion of 'sustainable building', the most pertinent architectural ethos of today. We should not conceive of buildings as having to stand the test of time, but as conspicuously and intentionally failing that test. We should engage with the disappearance of buildings as readily and enthusiastically as we do their creation, and explore the infinite gains that present themselves. Plan for obsolescence! Once again, the life of an architect could be straightforward: stop designing new buildings, focus on adapting existing ones; if the need for a new building becomes inescapable, conceive of its ending as much as of its coming into being.

All that is built will have to be demolished at one point; but all that is manufactured merely has to be taken apart. Demolition produces debris; disassembly implies the possibility of reassembling the components elsewhere. The Palast der Republik lives on in Burj Khalifa. The prefabricated elements of Großsiedlung Marzahn live on in the inconspicuous family homes of Brandenburg. The seat of the European Council is built from the combined debris of demolished EU buildings. Modern construction craves these types of reincarnation but rarely gets them.

Imagine: The source material of buildings no longer comes from the extraction of resources but from infinite recycling. Traditional supply chains, reliant on months of material procurement and shipping, become obsolete. Building materials are no longer imported from remote parts of the planet but are taken from dismantled structures nearby.

A limitless number of new combinations and permutations emerge from existing elements – dusted off, polished, swiped, packaged and teleported into a new life. We don't build; we don't demolish. Construction and demolition merge into the single category of permanent conversion. No physical reality is ever final.

The construction industry as we know it is gone. The traditional contractor is an ancient relic, his business a race against irrelevance. Building has become a continuous, automated process. Construction sites are no longer recognizable as such – transformed into laboratory environments, clean to the point of sterility. AI-driven design directly feeding into 3D printing eliminates any distinction between inception and execution. The end of that distinction also conveniently marks the end of opposing sides. All legal battles end here. The role of human labour has become negligible. Automated construction swarms and robotic assemblers are controlled from the tiniest of control rooms. AI-driven cranes and autonomous drones erect massive buildings in mere hours.

Just as rapidly as they are built, they are deconstructed. Buildings last no longer than tents, IKEA furniture or Japanese tatami. A building ready by sunrise is gone by dusk, its materials reprocessed into a new building ready the next morning. Waste is a non-issue, as are cultural heritage and preservation policies. Any notion of permanence is nullified. Building technology evolves at a horrifying speed. By the time any structure nears completion, superior alternatives have already come into being. Innovation has made its way back into architecture, with each new innovation driving down the cost of earlier ones. Just like cars, refrigerators and computers, buildings naturally depreciate. People are able to buy a second-hand home for a second-hand price. The affordability crisis ends here! Property speculation is a thing of the past. No longer will we be running an economy rooted in the artificial inflation of debt. *L'immobilier devient mobile.*

Structures will weigh next to nothing; there to be dropped, lifted and moved at will. Concrete or steel foundations are but a distant memory – no more than ancient anchors in the way of global impermanence. Stand-alone micro-reactors and ultra-thin photovoltaic skins provide power on demand, eliminating any need for energy grids. Water and waste systems are embedded within walls. Conventional plumbing is a thing of the past, as is the concept of fixed HVAC systems: temperature and airflow are regulated in real-time, in line with the latest weather forecast. Buildings will become footloose, just like people. The built environment will exist in a perpetual state of flux. There is no skyline to admire, no enduring landmarks – only a shimmering, ever-reconfiguring urban condition where all material reality is in a state of becoming. Cities will be no more permanent than army camps, that other quintessential Roman area of expertise. Fuller's journey towards 'ephemeralization' may end how it began.

13

Forget Sustainability

I was born in the Netherlands in 1964 – about ten years after the country had been hit by a major catastrophe. A combination of spring tide and a north-westerly storm had caused sea levels to rise more than 4 metres above normal and 200,000 hectares of land were flooded. Three of the southern provinces were severely affected, including the one where I lived. Nearly 2,000 people died and over 100,000 were evacuated. More than 45,000 buildings were damaged, 10,000 of which were completely destroyed.

Memories of the disaster were still fresh. I remember family conversations, particularly between my grandparents, about how dangerously close the water had come to Rotterdam, and how they, too, had been alerted to the possibility of evacuation. But the dikes guarding the city from the water held and Rotterdam was spared. Such stories scared me. Two thirds of my country was below sea level, with our home squarely in the middle. Still, I was assured that in my lifetime I would never experience such a danger. Major engineering works had started almost immediately after the flooding. As part of the Deltaplan, estuaries were closed off, dikes were raised and strengthened, and an ingenious system of storm surge barriers with open sluices was built across the Eastern Scheldt delta. The all-out approach was to ensure that the Netherlands would never have to face the same disaster again.

A decade after the storm, most of these works were well under way. A sense of pride prevailed. More than a reaction to the disaster, the Delta Works were an act of defiance. My father took me to see the construction work on the Haringvlietdam built to regulate the waterflow between the North Sea and the rivers Rhine and Meuse. The scenes were impressive: huge cranes, like the skeletons of monsters trying to reach for the sky, dredging vessels scrounging at their feet, industrious colonies of trucks and bulldozers busy moving about rock and sand, and machines pouring concrete, infinite amounts of concrete. I could see the sluices and roadworks taking shape. The dam was nearing completion. One of many, ready to withstand any future storm. We could relax. The Netherlands had survived. Defiant, but not unscathed. Farmers struggled with salination, the saltwater having sunk deep into the soil. And there were other problems too: fishermen were put out of business due to the change in tidal flows; rural areas were left vacant as people flocked to the big cities in search of work; and temporary barracks would continue to house the displaced until the mid-1980s. But at the time these seemed minor concerns. The forces of nature had been tamed, or at least competently kept at bay. We did not need to worry about them in the same way ever again. For now, that was all that mattered.

❧

Does human behaviour impact climate change? Misinformation aside, the overwhelming majority of scientists find that it does. The question is whether that matters at this point. Even if humans didn't impact climate change, climate change meanwhile dramatically impacts humans. Increasingly so. Already the costs of dealing with the consequences are affecting the global economy to a worrying degree. The World Meteorological Organization has estimated that between 2010 and 2019 extreme weather events caused worldwide losses of $1.4 trillion.

At the Paris climate change conference in 2015, world leaders agreed to limit global warming to 1.5°C by 2100. To achieve that, emissions would have to be halved by the end of the present decade. If no changes are made, the planet will heat up by 4°C by 2100, causing yet more storms, deadly heatwaves and the flooding of coastal cities due to polar ice melt.[1]

The signs aren't hopeful. Declarations following climate summits tend to be a litany of petty excuses, generally outlining the reasons why the targets of the previous summit have not been met. 'No agreement is perfect.'[2] 'Climate action knows no quick fixes.'[3] 'All things considered, we have made reasonable progress but it is not enough.'[4] Political action on climate change is failing by its own admission.

The recent tendency to put national interests first isn't helping. 'I was elected to represent the citizens of Pittsburgh, not Paris.' A year after the Paris Agreement had come into force, Donald Trump announced the US's withdrawal from it as a 'solemn duty to protect America and its citizens'.[5] On the occasion of India's presidency of the G20, Prime Minister Modi, in a thinly veiled attempt to lobby for the transfer of finance and technology to India, urged a 'more constructive attitude to climate change'. Meanwhile, in stating that China's 'path, method, pace and intensity to achieve [climate goals] should . . . never be influenced by others', Chinese President Xi Jinping basically told everyone else to mind their own business.[6]

Ironically perhaps, the increasing reluctance to enter into international cooperation is partly fuelled by the real-time workings of climate change itself. No matter how much climate change is portrayed as a global threat, the radical consequences predicted turn out to be radically different for different parts of the world. While Pacific Island nations are rapidly disappearing into the ocean, Northern Siberia and Canada eagerly await new agricultural opportunities and the benefits of northern shipping routes. The future of the one is hopeless, that of the other hopeful.

In a world where more and more countries are focusing primarily on themselves, banking on global solidarity is a dangerous gambit. As has been all too evident from recent events. At the time of writing, the US is (once again) pulling out of the Paris Agreement and has announced plans to extract more oil from its own soil. The US president has also expressed an interest in purchasing Greenland from Denmark (as a matter of US national security), while his counterpart in Russia is musing over its citizens having to spend less on fur coats. It seems that the most direct response to climate change is not a global acceptance of self-sacrifice but rather a collective run on the world's remaining resources, regardless of whether their consumption contributes to further global warming or not. The Cold War arms race finds its twenty-first-century successor in a race to the Arctic. When it comes to climate change, united we do not stand. The worst may be yet to come.

Climate change has long been a concern for architects, as it should be. The construction industry is the largest source of CO_2 emissions globally. Although only peripherally involved in the emissions of CO_2 itself, the architecture profession is no less caught in the crossfire. The mission statements of architecture firms invariably convey their deep commitment to the cause of sustainability. Driven by a sense of guilt perhaps, architects tend to underpin that commitment by acting as flag bearers for a whole series of so-called 'improved practices': 'net zero', 'triple zero', 'carbon neutrality', 'zero carbon', 'climate positivity', 'eco-friendliness', 'green growth', 'circularity' . . . the sheer proliferation of terms cancels out the validity of each.

The same applies to the systems introduced to evaluate their success. BREEAM, LEED, WELL, SKA, Casa Clima, Passivhaus, ILFI, Beam Plus, HQE, Minergie, Green Globes, CASBEE, The Green Building Initiative, the Living Building Challenge, EDGE, G-SEED, Green Star, SITES, Fitwel, Envision, Earth Check . . . A plethora of sustainability certificates promote a selective, tick-box approach that fosters a false sense of security. The extent of each checklist deflates whatever urgency they are trying to convey. The contemporary architect is like a firefighter required to check the industrial compliance of his firehose inside a burning house.

Each certificate stems from the same ambition, or rather, from the same delusion: that climate change can be mitigated to the point that it won't *really* affect the practices of construction. Words like 'revolution' or 'paradigm shift' may suggest drastic changes in terms of construction methods, but that is largely a form of grandstanding. Most of what we are seeing amounts to a slightly improved version of business as usual.

Given the vested interests at stake, that should hardly come as a surprise. Sustainability policies are co-scripted with market actors at a global scale – the same actors that the policies seek to contain. Make no mistake: the real objective of sustainability is the sustaining of current practice – at all costs.

The construction industry is notoriously resistant to change, and it has been able to cultivate that resistance through the invention of its own idiosyncrasies and semantic twists. Language is key. Euphemisms pervade the glossary of building to its very core. Each 'radical transformation' masks the de facto absence thereof. The carbon footprint of construction is anything but 'zero'; there is nothing 'friendly' about its relation to the ecosystem, nor is there anything 'positive' about its impact on the climate.

The catchy ring of terms like 'net zero' or 'carbon neutrality' stands in stark contrast to their impact in the real world. The 2022 Buildings-GSR found that

> despite a substantial increase in investment and success at a global level lowering the energy intensity of buildings, the sector's total energy consumption and CO_2 emissions increased in 2021 above pre-pandemic levels. Buildings energy demand increased by around 4 per cent from 2020 to 135 EJ – the largest increase in the last 10 years. CO2 emissions from buildings operations have reached an all-time high of around 10 GtCO2, around a 5 per cent increase from 2020 and 2 per cent higher than the previous peak in 2019.[7]

The same applies to the prevailing obsession with timber construction. Here too, the numbers invalidate the rhetoric.

Substituting the yearly 14 billion cubic metres of concrete with wood requires three times more than what we currently harvest. A good yield of wood is judged to be 35 metric cubes per hectare; to match the 14 billion, we would have to plant 265 million hectares of forest every year, an area slightly smaller than Argentina. Given that a tree has to be at least forty years old to be usable for construction, the area would not be fully productive until 2065.

And then there is the fascination with building in space. Recently we've seen projects for the Moon as well as Mars. In collaboration with the European Space Agency, the Australian architecture firm Hassell has developed a 'Lunar Masterplan' for 'a scalable habitat for 144 people in reduced gravity';[8] Foster + Partners have been working on a NASA-backed competition for a 3D-printed modular habitat on Mars;[9] and BIG has launched (pun intended) 'Mars Science City', a prototypical test site in Dubai for a sustainable city on Mars. The project is legitimized as a general rehearsal for when we eventually go to Mars – in BIG prose: 'a Martian embassy on earth, the first foothold of our neighbor on Terran soil'.[10]

Notwithstanding the sponsorship of European and American space agencies for such ideas (no doubt with major political and private backing), one cannot help but wonder: are we seeing a general rehearsal for life on Mars, or are we witnessing the announcement of a future life on a similarly uninhabitable Earth? Controlled climates, artificial gravity, human-made ecosystems? Mars today, Earth tomorrow?

Hurricanes, floods, heatwaves, forest fires . . . The more the realities of climate change manifest, the more the futility of current architectural approaches becomes apparent. Sustainability efforts in the hope of avoiding the worst are unconvincing. As are phantasmagorical projects in outer space. We can neither avert nor escape the consequences of climate change. What is needed is a major shift in thinking.

Any such shift should begin with the frank acknowledgement that architecture in its present form is subject to an unresolvable conflict of interest. Buildings are both the largest repository of global capital and the biggest source of carbon emissions – at once the most important pillar of the global economy and the biggest threat to the globe. The dual nature of buildings is representative of the broader conflict that exists within our societies as a whole: the conflict between the sustenance of our livelihood and that of the living world, between the contradictory imperatives of economy and environment. More plainly, between capital and (the fight against) climate change.

Both capital and climate change find their origin in the extraction of the Earth's resources for human subsistence (and their eventual conversion into wealth), yet they attribute a vastly different normative charge to that process: to the benefit of humanity in the logic of the first, to its detriment in that of the latter. The type of human relations implied by each concept – relations both of humans to each other and of humans collectively to the Earth – couldn't be more different. One demands competition, the other presumes cooperation; one preaches individualism, the other pleads solidarity; one fosters growth, the other urges moderation; one asks of us that architects continue at an accelerated pace, the other that they stop.

The problem with the mitigation strategies currently practised by the construction industry – and thus by architects – is that they are not so much an attempt to resolve this conflict as they are a way of wilfully prolonging it. The prevailing focus on 'process improvement', 'energy-efficient design' and 'green building methods' mostly amounts to business slightly better than usual, never really questioning the nature of business itself.

It is an illusion to think that more responsible design or execution of the same buildings will exorcise the fundamental conflict embedded within them. To resolve this conflict architects will have no choice but to move beyond building. The current exclusive focus on buildings only highlights further the inherently schizophrenic nature of our profession.

Just as we need to move beyond building, we should also move beyond the moral charge we attribute to it. The whole idea that our work might somehow change the outcome, impact or severity of climate change is a form of self-delusion. Buildings do not alter the nature of climate change; climate change alters the nature of building.

As Ernest Becker wrote, 'Mother Nature is a brutal bitch, red in tooth and claw, who destroys what she creates.'[11] For the next 100 years or so, humankind will live under the dictatorship of the planet. The prevailing notion that we must combat climate change in order to save the world or preserve nature is nothing short of human hubris. We cannot mitigate climate change; we have no choice but to adapt to it and explore meaningful ways to coexist with the inevitable. Nature is neither an ideal condition that we must keep intact, nor an adversary that we must keep at bay. Nature will go on – even if we don't. Humanity doesn't command nature; it is part of nature. Let's not kid ourselves: there is no moral dimension to us battling climate change other than the drive for self-preservation – the ingrained instinct to survive, which, ultimately, is a simple fact of nature too.

If we accept that humanity is part of nature, then, by deduction, the same applies to the processes that humanity initiates: they ought to be viewed as an extension of natural processes. By that measure, everything created by humans – cities, technologies, infrastructures – is inevitably a continuation of the Earth's dynamic systems. As is their fallout. Waste, emissions, pollution . . . even climate change itself.

From the largest metropolis to the most extensive rainforest, in the Anthropocene *all* environments are built environments. 'Nature' is as much a constructed reality as the city is an evolving ecosystem. That realization compels us to radically rethink what we occupy ourselves with as a profession. When all environments are built environments, it is inevitably the notion of building itself that changes most fundamentally. No longer do we build at the expense of the unbuilt – construct something where there was nothing – rather, the act of building becomes one of permanent mediation. There are no virgin conditions, only pre-existing ones. We perpetually intervene in situations with an evolving logic of their own. Each act of building is simply the next intervention in a long series.

In that context, more than a wilful act of creation, architecture becomes an act of calculated manipulation. Whether it is the adaptation of existing structures, the transformation of urban environments in the name of enhancing liveability, the domestication of large tracks of the countryside, or the rewilding of former farmlands in response to the ever more virulent forces of nature . . . architecture begins wherever the presumption of authenticity ends. The fundamental revolution of architecture is the realization that all nature is architecture and that all architecture is nature.

To stay relevant in the age of climate change, the architecture profession must drastically escalate its remit. No longer can it afford to be an insular domain exclusively dedicated to the creation of buildings (sustainable or otherwise); it must preoccupy itself at a scale it rarely encounters. Cities, roads and infrastructure – the largest scale at which our profession currently operates (in the form of urbanism) – only cover between 1 and 3 per cent of the Earth's surface. Escalating our involvement to the totality of the Earth's surface will mean urging architecture to reinvent itself as a completely new discipline. From an inward-looking bastion of creative individuals, it must evolve into a comprehensive field of knowledge – not an applied art but a natural science.

Any such reinvention lands architecture with unprecedented responsibilities. Even more than at present, the complexities involved will make architects dependent on the knowledge of others. 'Science now finds there can be ample for all, but only if the sovereign fences are wholly removed', wrote Richard Buckminster Fuller in 1969.[12] No doubt, he was talking about the fences between nations, but today we could equally apply Fuller's statement to the fences that separate our metier from technology and science. There is a world of knowledge to be acquired about the processes at work in what we formerly considered the unbuilt; at the same time, we will have to rethink everything we *thought* we knew about the built. To gain ground we must concede ground.

Architecture as we knew it was a discipline dedicated to the idea of control; architecture reinvented will make any such notion impossible. The conquest of a new scale and scope must inevitably coincide with the complete surrender of any idea of power over either. More than ever, architecture will be a mix of omnipotence and impotence.

'We are like a surfer on the waves; he doesn't control them, but he knows them.'[13] This simile from OMA's *S,M,L,XL* calls out the myth of architectural mastery over the urban condition. At a planetary scale, the same applies in the extreme. Even more than the city, the environment is an authorless condition. Its manifestation is the default sum of all processes at work, including our own. All we may hope for is to know and understand these processes, either by studying them, or by studying the effects of our interventions.

In architectural terms, 'the environment' can be viewed as a work of construction by an unknown author whose work we must inherit with a mix of respect and disbelief – not unlike the state of mind we adopt for the conversion of an old monument. We do not start from scratch; rather we act like surgeons asked to operate on the human body. The first steps are to establish the extent of the treatment necessary, the likelihood of its success, and the possible side effects.

Like medicine, architecture has become a matter of life and death. The wrong building in the wrong place can cause severe casualties. Yet, despite similar levels of urgency, the approaches of the two fields remain decidedly different. Where medicine is driven by rapid action and iterative reflection, architecture is stuck in extended reflection and deferred action. Medicine is subject to a continuous feedback loop of real-time examination, diagnosis and intervention; architecture insists on the separation between thinking and doing. Medicine involves hands-on training; architecture is locked in a fruitless antagonism between theory and praxis. Architecture focuses on the finite product; the work of a doctor is never finished.

That brings us to the other major paradigm shift climate change has in store for architecture. Unlike medicine, architecture is fixated on permanence, as pointed out in Chapter 12. The idea of building for eternity is deeply ingrained in the consciousness of our discipline. Even the modern movement, in its pursuit of ideal functional prototypes, adhered to the notion. Laudable as the aspiration may be, the reality is that in the age of climate change nothing can be permanent. Any conventional notion of architecture becomes moot. The Vitruvian triad of durability, functionality and 'timeless' beauty is not merely untenable but counterproductive.

'Things will endure less than us. Every generation must build its own city', wrote the futurist architect Antonio Sant'Elia in 1914.[14] For Sant'Elia that was hardly a bad thing. The Italian Futurist viewed destruction, even war, as a powerful source of progress. War was a purifying force, necessary to rid society of its weaknesses, old institutions and stagnant traditions.

How different is the reality of climate change from that of war? What will life on Earth look like after the icecaps have melted, sea levels have risen, the Gulf Stream has come to a standstill and the Earth's temperature has increased by 1.5, 2.5, 4 or even 6 degrees?

Think of it: weather perturbations have become the norm, seasons but a distant memory. Storms defy the categories used to classify them. Air travel amounts to Russian Roulette. Not land but 'wetland' is the prevailing texture of continents. Extremes are all that remain: floods and droughts, storms and fires. Evacuations are standard procedure, rescue and rebuild missions routine operations. Food shortages equally affect the Global South and North. The label 'climate refugee' can apply to anyone, anywhere, any time. Migration is the norm. Instant communities, makeshift nations . . . Humanity is 'mobilized' without exception. An 8.5-billion-strong army is left with no opposing force other than the force of nature.

An unruly world of rapidly changing fortunes . . . Climate change is exactly what it professes to be: *change*. Contrary to common portrayals, it does not represent the transition of one stable state to another, slightly more problematic state. Rather, climate change is like a nuclear chain reaction: a process that, once unlocked, cannot be stopped – one that will continue to evolve, continue to destabilize, forcing us to adjust, time and again, to radically different circumstances.

Impromptu settlements; designated habitable zones, shifting from region to region; roads like military supply routes, temporary tracks laid down where needed, more often than not replaced by drones altogether; pontoon bridges spanning rivers only for as long as needed; housing like army barracks, designed for rapid disassembly, movable at short notice; floating cities, shifting with floodwaters and tides . . . the only stable state of climate change is the state of emergency. Nothing can be taken for granted. All environments are built environments; all environments must be ready to be abandoned. Durability, functionality, beauty . . . Can climate change be the purifying force that rids architecture of its stagnant traditions?

Once more, an old declaration of Archigram becomes pregnant with meaning: 'If the shifting of things is characteristic of our time, we can do two things. We can dig our heels in, looking for absolutes and making rules, or we can ride the situation and try to chart a course that capitalizes on the shifts of events and values. Question, anticipate, combine, the like with the unlike.'[15] The future of architecture is both all-encompassing and all-fleeting. We had better make the most of it.

The dikes held, as did the promise. Throughout my life, I've never had to worry about my home being flooded or indeed the consequences of any other type of natural disaster. The Deltaplan's last storm surge barrier was completed on 10 May 1997, forty-four years after the Great Flood. At the barrier's opening, the Dutch queen spoke the historic words that the Netherlands were finally safe. It was hardly the end of things. The Delta Works were completed at a cost of €5 billion;[16] the cost of keeping the coastal defences adequate until 2050 has been estimated at €33 billion.[17] But the works didn't stop the water from striking again, this time from within. In 1995, severe inland river flooding led to the evacuation of 250,000 people – two-and-a-half times the number of evacuations in 1953.

In 2006, the Netherlands drastically changed course. A new water management strategy was implemented. Where the Deltaplan had focused on keeping seawater out with hard infrastructure like dams, dikes and storm barriers, the new approach was a calculated concession of territory to the water, in the form of giant floodplains and water storages. No cranes this time, and no steel or concrete either. The new engineering works were built with water and soil. If the Deltaplan had been the outspoken offensive, the new approach was a quiet revolution. No celebration of national pride, but every bit as radical and ambitious. Flood management would never be the same.

And the revolution doesn't stop there. Slowly but surely, an alternative approach to urban planning is also taking shape, with floating homes, artificial mounts and amphibious building structures that rise with the water levels. No longer do buildings claim to mitigate climate change; they adapt to it. The progressive insight that applied to dikes and dams equally applies to designing our habitat – not an act in defiance of nature, but a well-negotiated surrender.

14

On Whose Terms?

Gian Lorenzo Bernini was angry. The letter he'd received earlier that morning had left him exasperated. Once again, he had been called to travel to the Royal Court in Paris. Once again, it was on account of his work on the extension of the Louvre. The letter politely invited him to attend a review of his progress to date. Or rather, the lack thereof. He had drafted two proposals thus far and both had been rejected – the first for its supposed lack of attention to practical needs, the second for no apparent reason.

It was Colbert, the French Minister of Finance, who had been tasked with writing to him. Evidently, the king himself could not be bothered. He never knew whether he was in or out of favour with the young monarch. Nor did he much care. Throughout his long career he had become all too aware that there was a difference between men of noble blood and men of taste. As an artist, you were lucky if you found the two in one; more often they were worlds apart.

Louis XIV was an enigma. Allegedly, it had been *le Roi Soleil* himself who had insisted on the Italian's involvement, but only after the pool of every French architect of note had been exhausted. Then, when he finally received the commission, he had barely been allowed to finish his work and was asked to make changes practically upon submission. The faults found with the building were more numerous than the stones needed to build it.

The French envoy sent to Rome to escort him the first time had given ample warning. Louis XIV was no conventional patron of the arts; he was something else, incomparable even to other royalty. The king was not in the habit of waiting patiently for what he would be presented with; he was an artist in his own right, one who exercised the royal privilege to work through others. Being an artist, he did not approve plans any more than he rejected them; he simply changed his mind.

His praise in no way guaranteed seamless progression to the next stage. No more did his scorn guarantee cancellation. With Louis XIV, you never knew: were you in favour, out of favour, fired or hired? His young age notwithstanding, the king was known for his sudden lapses of memory, but nobody knew if these were real or conveniently feigned. His opinions could change at any time of day (or night). To rule in the absolute one had to be absolutely unpredictable.

Third time lucky . . . It was the best he could hope for. Comments, favourable or not, had not provided any clear steer in the past and it was doubtful they would this time. Time and again, he had tried to explain his reasons – for the curvature of the facade, for the central pavilion, for its slightly greater height. It had all been to no avail. The king never gave a definitive answer to anything. Instead, he preferred to change the subject – to hunting, billiards, fencing, parlour games or whatever else took his fancy. Either that, or he inquired excessively about details completely irrelevant at this early stage of the work.

Why resist? Only unconditional surrender to his majesty's whims offered hope of a way forward. Given the nature of their relationship, the diligent execution of his suggestions, however tasteless or banal, might even take the aspiring artist-monarch by surprise. Only a pre-emptive strike could avert the imminent standoff with his patron. Who knows, the move might even shake up his own preconceived ideas of beauty. Could sublimity equal banality in the extreme? *Les extremes se touchent*? What did he have to lose? In case it didn't, the project could always be disclaimed as a reflection of its patron, unimaginative and unappreciative of genius.

He would go on to disparage his royal subject in multiple other works. In Louis XIV's portrait bust, commissioned shortly after his arrival in Paris, he intentionally lowered the king's forehead (a sign of his limited intelligence); in the equestrian statue of the king, commissioned after his return to Rome, he portrayed the monarch with a slight, Gioconda-like smile, as though the undisputed ruler were rejoicing over the glory he had accrued at the price of bloodshed. The third and final iteration of his Louvre plans was completed shortly before the end of his visit. Upon review, the French king showered them with praise – only to have them shelved forever.[1]

Architecture and power: the relation between them is an unrelenting source of discomfort. Whatever enmity Bernini may have felt towards his patron, his true feelings must be inferred from a few coded messages cautiously embedded in his artworks. When it comes to the true nature of their relation, the despot ruler and the great artist converge in a pact of silence. Bernini's works endure as unequivocal tributes – art in the absolute in support of absolute reign.

More than a century later, the French Revolution seemed to bring profound changes. Having been the mere articulation of undisputed power, architecture became an expression of its transience. As revolutionary movements swept across Europe, so did their counterparts in architecture and planning: the Utopian Socialists of Fourier and Owen, the Garden City movement, Red Vienna, the Deutscher Werkbund, extending well into the next century in the form of Russian Constructivism, the Bauhaus, the Italian Futurists, L'Esprit Nouveau, CIAM . . . 'agents of progress' in the context of massive societal upheaval.

We tend to remember the individuals better than their movements. That is particularly true of the twentieth century, during which the myth of the architect-hero emerged. We recall Frank Lloyd Wright as 'FLW', the flamboyant dandy; Le Corbusier was 'Corbu' in his world the way Greta Garbo was 'Garbo' in hers;[2] and a certain Maria Ludwig Michael Mies rebranded himself 'Mies van der Rohe' to live on as 'Mies'. Less is more!

To equate the character of these figures to the ideology of the movements that produced them would be an overstatement. Frank Lloyd Wright's pacifist views (in combination with his distaste for anything British) brought him close to advocating appeasement policies towards Germany and Japan; Le Corbusier, a self-professed 'revolutionary syndicalist', did not shy away from offering his services to the Vichy regime when the opportunity presented itself; and Mies only left Germany in 1938, after a considerable time spent trying to ingratiate himself with the Nazis, even going so far as to sign a motion of support for Hitler in August 1934.

Should architects boycott oppressive leaders? Do buildings help glorify their ideology? The dilemma continues to preoccupy the profession as we struggle to find answers. Telling are the responses of contemporary architects when quizzed on the subject:

'As much as I would enjoy working in a bubble where everybody agrees with me, the places that can really benefit from our involvement are the places that are further from the ideals that we already hold' (Bjarke Ingels on working for Bolsonaro). 'I am neither a moralist nor a geopolitical analyst. I'm an architect' (Wolf Prix on working in Crimea). 'Working under adversarial conditions could be seen as a plus because you're offering alternatives' (Thom Mayne on working in the Middle East). 'Certainly I question working anywhere, but my position as an architect is to work in the spirit of international civilization and cooperation. You have to make a contribution' (Steven Holl on working in China). 'Only an idiot would have turned down this opportunity' (Jacques Herzog on pretty much working everywhere).

There is something endearing about architects trying to ingratiate themselves with the powers that be, about their wilful disregard both for political correctness and for their politically incorrect patrons, about their unwavering belief that they're above it all, smart enough to beat the system at its own game. The arguments are invariably the same. In no particular order, there is the I'm-open-to-anything argument; the if-not-us-someone-else-will argument; the bring-good-to-bad-places argument; the let-them-too-see-the-light argument; the no-politics-here argument; the architecture-is-art argument; the engaging-is-better-than-not-engaging argument; and, most popularly, the fuck-you-all argument.

This last, despite its cavalier charm, has become somewhat hard to stand by. The condition of migrant workers on construction sites – particularly in the Middle East, host to the world's next big building boom after China – has brought the ethical question a lot closer to home. No longer is it politics in the abstract that is being debated – the yes-or-no of buildings having any political implications in the long run. This time it concerns the fate, here and now, of fellow human beings involved in the realizations of architects' creations – members of the project team, colleagues, even if few architects tend to think of them like that.

When, in 2009, Human Rights Watch asked the architecture firms involved in the design of Saadiyat Island in Abu Dhabi to publicly pledge that they had obtained guarantees from their respective development partners that the project 'will not be tainted by the prevalent practices of migrant worker abuse',[3] the answers given by most of them were deferential: AJN, after having been repeatedly pushed on the issue, stated that they had checked and found that workers had the same conditions, if not better, than those in other countries.[4] Gehry Partners' lawyer responded that the firm had been engaged in a substantial and ongoing dialogue over many years involving government, the construction industry, architects, sponsors and NGOs. Meanwhile Foster + Partners, via a spokesperson, defused the issue by stating that the firm was looking forward to working with their client to achieve 'their values in areas of sustainability, health and safety, labour practices and philanthropy'.[5]

The run-up to the 2022 Qatar World Cup brought matters to a head. In response to questions about her practice working on the Al Wakrah Stadium in Qatar, Zaha Hadid was quoted as saying that architects had 'nothing to do with workers who have died on construction sites'.[6] (When asked about these remarks during a BBC Radio 4 interview, she famously stormed out of the studio.) Where Hadid chose outright confrontation, Foster + Partners mostly dodged the issue, stating that the practice 'was only involved in the initial design concept development phase', and that 'enquiries regarding the welfare of workers engaged in the venue's building process are best addressed by the Supreme Committee for Delivery & Legacy, tasked with managing the workers' welfare program across all of Qatar's FIFA World Cup projects'.[7]

The Beijing Olympics in 2008 . . . The Qatar World Cup in 2022 . . . These days, it is mainly architects working in Saudi Arabia who are subject to ethical scrutiny. There is ample noise about it in the media. Mostly from commentators though. Quotes from architects themselves are hard to come by as their work is covered by extensive non-disclosure agreements. In the Neom exhibition at the 2023 Venice Biennale, architects were shown speaking on the black-and-white screens of stacked television sets. All spoke at length, but all spoke at the same time, making it impossible for the audience to hear what any of them had to say. The effect of too much talk equalling that of no talk – the perfect tribute to the gratuitous nature of their presence.

❧

For all its manifest incongruity, the recent construction boom in Saudi Arabia may be an early taste of what's in store. No longer is the professional authority of architects a given. In most of KSA's megaprojects, their involvement is incidental at best. The Line, the Cube, Oxagon, Trojena . . . each project involves a melee of different architects, but *the* architect remains conspicuously unknown. Working on these projects is like fusion cooking under the direction of a permanently absent master chef.

The design of each megaproject is a foregone conclusion. Intentionally so. The role of the architect is not to create projects but to substantiate them. Their 'input' must suggest a process behind what has otherwise emerged from thin air; portray as liveable a way of life that few might choose to live; promote as sustainable what is potentially detrimental to the Earth; and sell as place what can only ever be placeless. In the latest generation of Saudi projects, the role of architecture is a mix of marketing and validation, effective insofar as the credibility of architects goes, inevitably finite over time.

All design is tentative. Solutions can be adopted or discarded at will. Competitions are won only to be never heard of again, while other competitions are lost only to be ordered into immediate execution. Take it or leave it! The Kingdom develops on its own terms. All are welcome to join in, and if not, there are always others who will. Generous fees work miracles: just as China and India have disrupted global markets with their endless reservoir of labour, Saudi Arabia disrupts them with its endless reservoir of cash.

High-profile media campaigns emphasize the involvement of architects all over the world. At the same time, they make sure never to expose to what extent, on what part or at which stage of the process that involvement takes place. NDAs ensure no one gets hurt in the process – or at the very least prevent architects from losing themselves trying to justify, or even understand, the nature of their involvement.

The master creator, the independent author, the client's confidante, even the eccentric artist permitted to rely on charisma rather than reason . . . in the desert, all the architect's former identities bite the dust. Working in Saudi Arabia marks the definitive repositioning of the architect as a service provider. The role involves all aspects of their work, including the provision of their signature style. Especially their style, in fact.

The figure of the lone genius, fountainhead of human creativity and progress, personified by FLW in the twentieth century, finds a new lease of life in MBS in the twenty-first. All visions must give way to *his* vision. Absolute rule signals the absolute irrelevance of architects.

The Kingdom and its architects: the swansong of all former delusions of grandeur. There is no process, just the recipience of an endless series of random requests. There is no planning, only progressive insight. There are no convictions, only apologies. Just as there are no certainties, merely opinions (the architect's just one of many). The most detailed considerations coincide with the most arbitrary conceptual a priori. Rigour counts, as does wilfulness. Approval, rejection, rejection, approval, rejection . . . All to be taken in stride.

Saudi Arabia may seem an exotic, even quaint, place to many. Bedouin traditions go hand in hand with an insatiable appetite to modernize, managed by an energetic young royal with a fascination for modern technology – not quite your usual architects' work environment.

Still, we architects go where the work is and often that lands us well outside of our comfort zone. The exposure of our work processes to the workings of absolute rule is par for the course – but only temporarily. Saudi Arabia's radical transformation is an experiment, as is working there; both are conditioned and conditional – fun (and financially rewarding) while it lasts.

But how quaint is Saudi Arabia really? As I'm finishing this chapter, a press conference is being broadcast live from the Oval Office. Newly elected President Donald Trump and Elon Musk are outlining the latter's plans for streamlining US government services. Trump is sitting at his desk; Musk is standing, holding his infant son X. Trump wears a suit and tie; Musk wears a T-shirt and baseball cap. The breach of protocol is as flagrant as it is intentional. The president's special advisor is operating unelected and unchecked, a fact his disregard for dress code only serves to underline. The clumsy, seemingly improvised nature of the event does nothing to undo its message: the way things will be is the way they always were. No one gets between the eternal bond of power and wealth. The American electorate may never have to endure the ordeal of another election again.

Marching herds, military parades, exalted crowds, the hypnotic orator . . . The casually dressed, chit-chatting, ultra-high-net-worth individual is but the latest manifestation of unchecked power. Authoritarian rule indiscriminately finds its expression in entertainment and leisure. In the workplace, it comes in the form of brainstorm sessions, workshops and groupthink. After religion, 'fun' is now the opium of the people. The all-powerful tech-billionaire taking an interest in governance, or the governing royal with an interest in tech. Where, ultimately, is the difference? Musk or MBS? Who is emulating whom? Is Saudi Arabia catching up with us, or are we catching up with Saudi Arabia?

At a mesmerizing pace, the self-proclaimed centre of the free world is staging its own version of absolute rule. Less than a month into his second term, Trump intends to buy Greenland, reclaim the Panama Canal, turn Gaza into a luxury resort and hand Ukraine to Russia. *The Plot Against America* is unfolding in real time, in plain sight, leaving the rest of the world aghast. History makes a U-turn as all the grand narratives play out in reverse: progress is equated with its undoing; there is a newfound freedom in curbing the freedom of others; inequality is promoted in the name of egalitarianism; the over-privileged champion the rights of the under-privileged; and justice for all becomes equal to its abuse.

Even if no more than a detail in the grand scheme of things, among the freedoms curbed is the creative freedom of architects. In an executive order issued in January 2025, titled 'Promoting Beautiful Federal Civic Architecture', Trump decreed that 'federal public buildings should be visually identifiable as civic buildings and respect regional, traditional, and classical architectural heritage.'[8] Forced to comply with pre-established standards, architecture is enlisted in a wider war on progressive values in which beauty is synonymous with classicism, the civic with the traditional; in which the federal must adhere to a heritage it never had.

Trump's position on architecture marks a significant shift. Even if the notion of the all-powerful architect waned with the dismantling of the welfare state, there was still a significant degree of freedom for the architect to act as a mediator between private and public interests in the context of the market economy. This dual consideration – working for its source of income on the one hand and the greater good on the other – sets architecture apart from other liberal professions. Where doctors and lawyers are expected (within certain boundaries) to cultivate a singular loyalty towards their patients and clients, architecture by definition is a profession of conflicted loyalties.

The more the notion of 'the public' is equated with the prevailing powers, the more the role of the architect as a public servant takes on a perverse twist. Conflicting loyalties become taboo. From an act requiring the balancing of private and public powers, architecture becomes an act of power pure and simple. Once more, architecture is the word in stone. Yet it is hardly the word of the architect that is turned into stone. The power of architecture serves merely to reflect the power of whoever holds power.

As the distinction between the public and the personal gradually fades into the background, so does the distinction between the architect and their client. From a public servant, the architect turns into a private servant, the work limited by the favour of patrons, its course subject to extreme whims. Even the most 'objective' criteria of evaluation remain subject to personal interpretation, which may change at will. Trump's view on what makes a 'beautiful federal building' will no doubt prove as volatile as his personal friendships with certain foreign dictators – no more rational or predictable than the artistic judgement of an absolute monarch.

Starchitects collected like trophies in Saudi Arabia, or architects as the willing followers of Trump's prescribed federal style . . . World-famous artists, or anonymous functionaries of the powers that be . . . The difference might be smaller than one thought. One thing both identities have in common is that they are conveniently exempt from having to answer to the general public. Where one hides behind the client's instructions, the other refuses explanation in the name of art. None of it serves to mask the reality of the architect as an imploded figure. Ironically, it is exactly when architecture becomes art that it is at its most powerless. The anonymous professional and the world-class artist . . . In the end, they may simply be different manifestations of the same thing.

The fall of the Berlin Wall, followed by the dissolution of the Soviet Union, was supposed to pave the way for the universal triumph of liberal democracy and a level playing field globally – economically and politically. Three decades later, we see a very different political reality. Since the turn of the millennium, the number of established liberal democracies in the world has declined from 120 to seventy-four, fifty of which are officially categorized as flawed democracies.[9] Even if today there are more elections than there were before the fall of the Wall, in more and more of those elections the outcome is known in advance.

The announced 'post-political condition' did not mark the end of politics. No sooner was the power of ideology declared dead than the ideology of power returned. Insofar as there is a globally levelled playing field, it manifests in the form of a universal 'will to power'. All other wills – to belief, to meaning, to truth – are rendered moot. Principles, religious or otherwise, are invoked to serve the presumed gains they bring – Trump is no more conservative than he is religious; facts give way to 'opinions', and the smaller the differences between them, the louder they are voiced.

Enhanced political theatre scarcely serves to mask the increasing homogenization that is taking place across different political systems. Democracies, monarchies, (former) communist states, modern autocracies . . . All are intensely present, but somehow the distinctions don't register the same way. Commonplaces are the language of all political debate. 'Transparency' registers high on the agenda in both democracies and dictatorships; 'sustainability' is a core value of both progressive and regressive policies; 'diversity', 'equity' and 'inclusion' are championed by both business and politics (each waiting for the other to make a real move). 'World class' is the common ambition of all nations combined.

It has taken a quarter of the new century for the reality to sink in, but now it has, unequivocally: there are no good or bad countries. The true legacy of globalization is not global politics, or even global trade, but a world collectively beyond good and evil. As such, it is also definitively beyond explanation. Global instability coincides with unprecedented global economic gains. Wars, insurrections, natural disasters go hand in hand with record profits and booming stocks. The economy has never done better; real estate has never been more valuable. All warring parties are equally committed to peace! Nothing in the world adds up, yet it is rife with opportunity.

As the plot thickens, the dilemmas for architects abound. No longer does choosing where you will and will not work serve as proof of morality. Navigating the world à la carte in the hope of retaining a clean conscience is a hope in vain. The conclusion that follows is as obvious as it is banal: if our morality cannot come from where we work, it must come from what we work on and how we do it.

Can architecture have agency in a world seemingly devoid of it? The current situation doesn't look good. It seems we can either engage at the expense of making a difference or focus on making a difference at the expense of engaging. Neither is an appealing prospect. What's the alternative? Can architects seek engagement *and* make a difference – not one at the expense of the other, but both at once?

To get there, it seems crucial for architects, once again, to find a way to move beyond the interests of their clients. The king looking to display his grandeur, the president aiming to project his power, the corporate CEO wishing to express his vision, the crown prince hoping to secure his legacy, the ambitious mayor looking to put his city on the map, the billionaire patron of the arts eager to do whatever . . . ultimately their concerns are of no importance.

The recommendations outlined in the latter part of this book call for the reinvention of architecture as a force for the good on its own terms, irrespective of the wishes of its clients. Work not to have clients; have clients to work. Whether it be the liberation of architecture from artistic pretensions; a reengagement with users by refusing to deal with middlemen; a stop to new construction to force fairer conditions; an unconditional pardon for all things built; planning for obsolescence to counter wastefulness; or the urgent appeal to go beyond sustainability in the context of climate change – all of the courses advocated here concern distinct and familiar areas in which architecture could make a key difference. They can be implemented tomorrow, regardless of firm size, architecture style or reputation.

Revolutions begin with uncomfortable realizations, often about oneself. If indeed architecture is to be a force for the good, the individuals and businesses practising it should set a shining example. It is here that the issues identified in the first part of this book – the presumed eternal creative life of figureheads, the lack of collective recognition and reward, the pointless obsession with authorship, the resistance to technology, and the insistence on an outmoded separation of theory from practice – become a precondition for the second.

In the end, the two parts of this book are flipsides of the same coin. At a time when more and more architects are struggling to justify their continued relevance, few of them are willing to acknowledge the elephant in the room – the uncomfortable truth that the absence of a meaningful agenda for the future might stem from the antiquated nature of the profession itself.

Architecture finds itself at the forefront in a race against time. As both the largest harbour of capital and the biggest source of global greenhouse emissions, buildings are at once the main opportunity for change and the main obstacle in its way. As such, they embody the perfect contradiction: both the custodians of vested interests and the eligible revolutionary soldiers to overthrow them.

Could the same apply to architects? In an age marked by the expiry of both credible politics and tenable loyalties, architects are on their own. No longer can we hide behind the powers that be. No affiliation, not even to the cleanest form of politics, is going to resolve our conflicts for us.

Still architects go where their work leads them, serving royalty, corporate CEOs, benevolent dictators and eccentric billionaires alike. Without an agenda of its own, architecture's mission continues to be equated with that of its clients. It is time architects openly declare their aims and bite the hand that feeds them if necessary.

There are more of us than ever, working in more countries, across more disciplines and more sections of society than at any previous point in history. Architects have the world as their playground, just as the world finds its playground in the international composition of architect practices. Our trade represents a unique body of knowledge – both about the globe and about globalization. Our utter dependence on the powers that be provides us with intimate knowledge of those powers. We must use that knowledge. The time has come for architecture to go beyond building and become a form of politics in its own right. This manifesto hopes to offer a small contribution.

Conclusion

Contemplating change is easy, forging change is not. The subject matter of this book is no exception. The world depends as much on construction as construction depends on the world. There is no way to reform the construction industry without also triggering seismic changes in other domains. A stop to new building would leave a massive workforce that would need to be retrained; recalibrating global built substance to the global population is impossible without massive expropriations; the ephemeralization of real estate cannot take place without grave risk to the financial system; and the pre-emptively mobile nature of human settlement, possibly across continents, would require a level of global solidarity unseen in history.

There is no underestimating the force of the vested interests in the way of meaningful change. I'm under no illusions. If architects decided to stop designing new buildings tomorrow, the world would surely not stop building them; it will take more than a pardon of the built environment to stop the wrecking balls; architecture will be art as long as there are those willing to regard it as such; few contractors will be lining up to employ architecture students; eternity will haunt the act of building as long as buildings continue to appreciate in value; and climate change will be paid lip service as long as the economy allows us to get away with it. The powers that be are such for a good reason.

End the focus on figureheads; welcome labour unions; collectivize practice; retire at sixty-seven; abolish authorship; rely on AI for matters of taste; end the distinction between theory and practice; free architecture from the concept of art; connect with users, cut out the middlemen; stop building until the existing stock runs out; pardon all things built; plan for obsolescence; adapt to climate change, stop claiming to mitigate it; work not to have clients, have clients to work!

Each of the fourteen recommendations in this book makes perfect sense; each recommendation in this book can be dismissed as perfectly impossible to implement. In the real world, both the political power and popular sway of architecture are limited. Still, one wonders: does the lack of likely implementation raise questions about the recommendations, or does the self-evident nature of each recommendation raise questions about their combined lack of implementation?

Any major change starts with one small step. Not too long ago, the US oil giants ExxonMobil and Chevron faced rebellion from activist shareholders over the companies' (lack of) plans for a low-carbon future. At Exxon, an activist hedge fund successfully staged a coup in which two Exxon board members were replaced; at Chevron, a proposal from an activist campaign group triggered a 61 per cent majority vote in favour from general shareholders. Both companies have drastically cut their carbon emissions since.[1]

The world's twenty largest construction companies build most of the large-scale, high-value infrastructure projects, public buildings, factories and office buildings around the world. Their revenue combined would easily rank them in the top twenty richest countries in the world. China State Construction Engineering alone, the largest of them all, has a yearly income the size of Finland's GDP. Even a small seat at the table of any of these might have consequences beyond our wildest imagination. Is it too far-fetched to imagine that what activist shareholders have achieved at Exxon and Chevron might also be possible in the construction industry? No one needs an architect to realize a building, yet no building is the same without an architect. Architecture does not invent building; it invents consciousness. Could our discipline reemerge as a form of conscientious activism?

Let architecture be architecture. Let architects go about their business. But let's also remember that ultimately all is political.

Notes

Architecture Against Architecture: A Manifesto

1. R. Buckminster Fuller, *Operating Manual for Spaceship Earth*, Carbondale: Southern Illinois University Press, 1969.

1. Firms, Not Founders

1. Will Ing, 'Obama and Bono Congratulate David Adjaye on RIBA Gold Medal Award', architectsjournal.co.uk, 27 May 2021.
2. Thelma Golden, 'David Adjaye', time.com, 2017.
3. UK Cabinet Office, *New Year's Honours 2017: Overseas and International List – Higher Awards Notes*, London: Cabinet Office, 2017, 2.
4. Ing, 'Obama and Bono Congratulate David Adjaye on RIBA Gold Medal Award'.
5. Adjaye Associates, 'The Abrahamic Family House', adjaye.com.

6. Josh Spero and Anjli Raval, 'Sir David Adjaye: The Celebrated Architect Accused of Sexual Misconduct', ft.com, 4 July 2023.
7. Ibid.
8. Alex Marshall, 'David Adjaye Relinquishes Roles After Reported Accusations of Misconduct', nytimes.com, 4 July 2023.
9. Dan Howarth, 'Adjaye "Embarrassed as a Male" That Women Still Need to Fight for Gender Parity', dezeen.com, 23 January 2017.
10. The Architecture Foundation, 'Sir David Adjaye: Making Memory', youtube.com, 18 February 2019.
11. Will Hurst, Anna Highfield and Richard Waite, '"The Cult of David": Former Adjaye Associates Employees Speak Out as Practice Cuts Staff', architectsjournal.co.uk, 14 September 2023.
12. Ibid.
13. Pritzker Architecture Prize, 'Jury Citation: Kevin Roche', pritzker prize.com.
14. Pritzker Architecture Prize, 'Jury Citation: Gottfried Böhm', pritzkerprize.com.
15. Pritzker Architecture Prize, 'Jury Citation: Christian de Portzamparc', pritzkerprize.com.
16. Pritzker Architecture Prize, 'Jury Citation: Renzo Piano', pritzker prize.com.
17. Wikipedia, 'List of Skidmore, Owings & Merrill Buildings', en.wikipedia.org.
18. Ibid.

2. Architects, Unite!

1. Nate Berg, 'Inside Architectural Workers United', fastcompany.com, 7 July 2023.
2. See architecturalworkersunited.org.

3. IAMAW Local Lodge 2021, 'About', iamawdlw2021.com.
4. Ibid.
5. Isabella Breda, 'Everett Boeing Employees Vote on Union Contract Proposal', heraldnet.com, 13 October 2023.
6. Alex Fitzpatrick, 'Amazon Workers Vote Against Forming Union', time.com, 15 January 2014.
7. The Architecture Lobby, 'Green New Deal Working Group', architecture-lobby.org.
8. The Architecture Lobby, 'About', architecture-lobby.org.
9. The Architecture Lobby, 'Unionization Working Group', architecture-lobby.org.
10. Chris Walton, 'Workers at Snøhetta Vote Against Unionization', archpaper.com, 7 July 2023.
11. Noam Scheiber, 'Architects at a Prominent New York Firm Drop Their Unionization Bid', nytimes.com, 4 February 2022.
12. Andy Bernheimer, quoted in Berg, 'Inside Architectural Workers United'.
13. Snøhetta, quoted in Walton, 'Workers at Snøhetta Vote Against Unionization'.
14. See 'Building Monticello', monticello.org.
15. Peggy Deamer, 'Our Best Organizer', averyreview.com, March 2023.
16. Ibid.
17. Ibid.
18. Ibid.
19. Matthew Stewart, 'Architectural Work Without the Architect', *Aggregate*, vol. 2, 2014, 112–13.
20. FinancesOnline, 'Number of Freelancers in the US', financesonline.com.
21. Consiglio Nazionale degli Architetti, *La Professione di Architetto in Italia 2021*, Rome: CNAPPC, 2021, 34.

22. Salvatore Peluso, 'Architettura, Precariato, Sfruttamento', lampoon.it, 6 January 2023.
23. Redazione Build News, 'Professione Architetto, Osservatorio CNAPPC-Cresme: Pochi Progetti e Molti Servizi', buildnews.it, 2 March 2016.
24. Architects' Council of Europe, *The Architectural Profession in Europe 2022: Sector Study*, Brussels: ACE, 2023, 16.
25. See ordredesarchitectes.be.
26. Ordre des Architectes Belgique, *Le Statut Social du Stagiaire Architecte (Indépendant ou Salarié)*, Brussels: Ordre des Architectes, 2020, 2.

3. Co-everything

1. See architexturez.net.
2. Ibid.
3. Graeme Nuttall, *Celebrating the 10th Anniversary of the Nuttall Review*, Cardiff: Employee Ownership Wales, 2022.
4. Norman Lamb, quoted in Graeme Nuttall, *Sharing Success: The Nuttall Review of Employee Ownership*, London: Department for Business, Innovation and Skills, 2012, 1.
5. Ibid., 5.
6. US Congress, SECURE 2.0 Act of 2022, Section 346: 'Worker Ownership, Readiness, and Knowledge', Washington, DC: 117th Congress, 2022.
7. See employeeownership.co.uk.
8. Georgina Hutton, 'Business Statistics', UK House of Commons Library, 11 November 2024.
9. Greg Pitcher, 'Another AJ100 Firm Becomes Employee-Owned', architectsjournal.co.uk, 17 June 2019.

10. Matt Hickman, 'Top 300 US Architecture Firms of 2023', architecturalrecord.com, 9 June 2023.
11. Edie Cohen, 'A Tribute to Art Gensler and the Monumental Impact of His Legacy', interiordesign.net, 6 December 2021.
12. Will Stephens, quoted in Will Ing, 'Employee Ownership: Who Really Wins?', architectsjournal.co.uk, 28 January 2022.
13. See cullinanstudio.com.
14. Marson Korbi, quoted in Natalie Donat-Cattin, 'Collective Processes. Re-Thinking Architecture', koozarch.com, 16 December 2022.

4 Time's Up!

1. Oscar Niemeyer, quoted in UNESCO, *The UNESCO Courier*, Paris: UNESCO Publishing, June 1992.
2. Oscar Niemeyer, quoted in Eduardo Graça, 'The Last of the Modernists', metropolismag.com, 1 June 2006.
3. Ibid.
4. Paul Goldberger, 'Architecture View: What Pritzker Winners Tell Us About the Prize', nytimes.com, 29 May 1988.
5. Nicolai Ouroussoff, 'For Niemeyer, It's a Jungle Out There', nytimes.com, 26 December 2007.
6. Bodo Kandner, quoted in Rainer Schüler, 'So Soll Potsdams Neues Bad Werden', maz-online.de, 17 December 2015. Translated from the German.
7. Björn Meding, quoted in ibid.
8. Oscar Niemeyer, quoted in Oliver Wainwright, 'Oscar Niemeyer: The Man Behind the Monuments', theguardian.com, 6 December 2012.
9. Ibid.

10. Oscar Niemeyer, quoted in Henry Chu, 'He's Still Shaping a Legend', latimes.com, 29 March 2005.
11. Mason Currey, 'Happy Birthday, Oscar Niemeyer!', metropolis mag.com, 15 December 2009.
12. Michael Kimmelman, 'The Last of the Moderns', nytimes.com, 15 May 2005.

5. Free for All

1. World Intellectual Property Organization, Berne Convention for the Protection of Literary and Artistic Works, Article 6bis.
2. Ibid., Article 2.
3. Ibid.
4. China Intellectual Property, quoted in Marcus Fairs, 'Zaha Hadid Building Pirated in China', dezeen.com, 2 January 2013.
5. Meiquan 22nd Century, quoted in ibid.
6. Zahi Hawass, quoted in Rory McCarthy, 'Egypt to Copyright the Pyramids and Antiquities', theguardian.com, 27 December 2007.
7. Auditorio de Tenerife, Image Rights of Auditorio de Tenerife, auditoriodetenerife.com.
8. Steve Jobs, quoted in Jack Purcher, 'The Apple Store's Distinctive Design & Layout Is Now a Registered Trademark', patentlyapple.com, 24 January 2013.
9. Ryan Abbott, quoted in Augusta Pownall, 'First Patent Applications Filed for Designs Created by AI', dezeen.com, 1 August 2019.

6. After Taste

1. See runwayml.com.
2. See testfit.io.

3. See archistar.ai.
4. Walter Benjamin, *The Work of Art in the Age of Mechanical Reproduction*, New York: Schocken Books, 1969, 4.

7. Flourish in the Field

1. See ucl.ac.uk.
2. See t-ads.org.
3. See icd.uni-stuttgart.de.
4. See tudelft.nl.
5. See ruralstudio.org.
6. See arcd.ku.edu.
7. See bluff.designbuildutah.org.
8. See tsoa.edu.
9. Vitruvius, *The Ten Books on Architecture*, Cambridge: Harvard University Press, 1914, Book I, Chapter I, 5.
10. Leon Battista Alberti, *The Architecture of Leon Batista Alberti in Ten Books*, London: 1755, 3.
11. Ibid.
12. Anne Stengel, 'Learning through Building Practice', in Philipp Oswalt (ed.), *Hannes Meyer's New Bauhaus Pedagogy*, Leipzig: Spector Books, 2021.
13. Gino Spocchia, 'Cost of Living Crisis: Can You Still Afford to Be an Architect in 2023?', architectsjournal.co.uk, 13 December 2022.
14. Statista, 'Average Salary per Week of a Subcontractor Worker in Construction in England and Wales as of September 2024, by Region', statista.com.
15. Payscale, 'Average Design Architect Salary in Netherlands', pay scale.com.
16. European Federation of Building and Woodworkers, 'The Netherlands: Check Wages and Working Conditions', constructionworkers.eu.

8. Faux Arts

1. Richard Meier.
2. Zaha Hadid.
3. Le Corbusier.
4. Renzo Piano.
5. Richard Rogers.
6. Peter Zumthor.
7. Bjarke Ingels.
8. Tadao Ando.
9. I. M. Pei.
10. Le Corbusier.
11. Santiago Calatrava.
12. Alvar Aalto.
13. Louis Kahn.
14. Arne Jacobsen.
15. Philip Johnson.
16. Walter Gropius, *Manifesto of the Staatliches Bauhaus*, Weimar: Staatliches Bauhaus, 1919.
17. Under current UK tax law, certain art pieces may be exempt from capital gains if classified as 'chattels' (a legal term from the Tudor period), while the UK's non-domiciled tax regime historically allowed residents who were not domiciled in the UK to avoid taxation on foreign income. In April 2025 the non-dom tax regime was abolished.
18. Karl Marx, *Capital: A Critique of Political Economy, Volume 1*, London: Penguin, 1990, 131.
19. Steve Rose, 'The House that £3m Built', theguardian.com, 6 February 2007.
20. Rupert Neate, 'The Gherkin sold to Brazilian billionaire Joseph Safra', theguardian.com, 10 November 2014.

21. Jeff Koons, *Puppy*, guggenheim-bilbao.eus, 1992.

9. For Us, By Us

1. Henry Frugès, quoted in Philippe Boudon, *Lived-in Architecture*, Cambridge, MA: MIT Press, 1972, 51.
2. Ibid., 8, 10, 9.
3. Interview with resident, quoted in ibid., 78.
4. Ibid., 81.
5. Ibid.
6. Ibid., 82.
7. Ibid., 102.
8. UNESCO, 'The Architectural Work of Le Corbusier, an Outstanding Contribution to the Modern Movement', whc.unesco.org, 2016.
9. Commune de Pessac, *Quartiers Modernes Frugès, Pessac, Gironde: Zone de Protection du Patrimoine Architectural, Urbain et Paysager*, 1997, preamble. Translated from the French.
10. Ibid.
11. Ibid.
12. Sud-Ouest, 'Cité Frugès Le Corbusier à Pessac: pourquoi la Région ne financera plus les rénovations des propriétaires privés', sudouest.fr, 21 November 2023.
13. Ville de Pessac, 'Mécénat', citefrugeslecorbusier.pessac.fr, 2023.
14. Le Corbusier, *Le Corbusier Talks with Students*, New York: Princeton Architectural Press, 1999, 26.
15. Urban.brussels, 'LA MÈME', archiweek.urban.brussels, 2023.
16. N. John Habraken, *Supports: An Alternative to Mass Housing*, London: The Architectural Press, 1972, 14.
17. Giancarlo De Carlo, 'An Architecture of Participation', *Perspecta*, vol. 17, 1980, 77.
18. Ibid., 79.

10. Stop Building, Now!

1. The slogan was first coined by President Xi Jinping in a speech at the annual meeting of the Central Economic Work Conference in Beijing in December 2016.
2. Louise Redvers, 'Angola's Chinese-Built Ghost Town', bbc.com, 3 July 2012.
3. Reinier de Graaf, *2008*, London: Machine Books, 2018.
4. Nqobile Dludla, 'South Africa's Redefine Says Property Cycle has Bottomed Out', reuters.com, 6 November 2023.
5. Charles Mwaniki, 'Office, Mall Rents Plunge on Jump in Space Supply', businessdailyafrica.com, 5 April 2022.
6. Abubakar Ibrahim, 'The Empty Mansions of Accra: 4 Perspectives on Unoccupied Luxury Homes', myjoyonline.com, 18 September 2024.
7. Amira El Masaiti, 'Over 1 Million Moroccan Homes Are Vacant, Mostly in Cities: HCP', moroccoworldnews.com, 3 October 2017.
8. Egyptian Streets, 'Egypt's Vacant Housing Units 12.8 Million: CAPMAS', egyptianstreets.com, 3 October 2017.
9. Rupert Neate, 'Scandal of Europe's 11m Empty Homes', the guardian.com, 23 February 2014.
10. HR NEWS, 'In 2024, America has 15.1 Million Vacant Homes While Homelessness Is at an All-Time High of 650,000 Human Beings without Housing', medium.com, 12 February 2024.
11. Ciara Nugent, 'Homes Empty and Tenants Homeless as Argentina's Peso Crisis Hits Rentals', ft.com, 20 December 2023.
12. BRIC Group, 'What the Latest Census Says about Housing in Brazil', bric-group.com, 18 July 2023.
13. Carl Glassman, 'To a Building, Emptiness Means Many Things', nytimes.com, 5 September 1976.

14. David Harvey, 'Senior Loeb Scholar Lecture, Harvard University Graduate School of Design', davidharvey.org, 28 March 2016.
15. Oliver Pieper, 'German Housing Crisis: "Like Winning the Lottery!"', dw.com, 16 April 2024.
16. Guy Chazan, '"Catastrophic" Outlook for German Construction Adds to Olaf Scholz's Woes', ft.com, 16 July 2023.
17. Pieper, 'German Housing Crisis'.
18. Statistischen Ämter des Bundes und der Länder, 'Zensus 2022: 1,9 Millionen Wohnungen am Zensusstichtag unbewohnt', zensus2022.de, 21 November 2023.
19. JLL, 'Office Market Dynamics Germany Big 7 – Q4 2024', jll.de, January 2025.
20. 293,000 in 2021 + 295,000 in 2022 + 294,000 in 2023 = 882,000 minus 3 x 400,000. MDR, 'Eure Geschichte: Wohnungswirtschaft und Städtebau nach 1990', mdr.de, 7 June 2022.
21. NL Times, 'Dutch Housing Shortage Rises to Over 400,000 as Population Growth Outstrips Construction', nltimes.nl, 12 July 2024.
22. Joëlle Baelde, 'Provincies gaan 900.000 nieuwe woningen bouwen', bnr.nl, 13 October 2022.
23. Ministerie van Binnenlandse Zaken en Koninkrijksrelaties, 'Aantal nieuwe woningen 2023 op peil', volkshuisvestingnederland.nl, 31 January 2024.
24. NOS, 'Meer bewoners in één woning, bouw extra etage en "minihuis" in strijd tegen woningnood', nos.nl, 17 May 2023.
25. John Campbell, 'Republic of Ireland "Needs 35,000 New Homes a Year"', bbc.co.uk, 2 July 2024.
26. Shauna Bowers, 'Number of Vacant and Derelict Homes Brought Back into Use for Social Housing Fell Last Year', irishtimes.com, 21 May 2024.
27. TPN/Lusa, 'Portugal Needs to Build "45,000 Homes per Year"', theportugalnews.com, 14 April 2024.

28. Neate, 'Scandal of Europe's 11m Empty Homes'.
29. The Brussels Times with Belga, '225,000 Additional Homes Needed by 2030 in Belgium', brusselstimes.com, 19 December 2023.
30. Jürg Zulliger, 'Von der Blasengefahr zur Wohnungsnot', nzz.ch, 20 March 2024.
31. Federal Statistical Office, 'Renewed Decline in the Dwelling Vacancy Rate in 2023', admin.ch, 11 September 2023.
32. Reuters, 'France Plans New Measures to Tackle Housebuilding Slump', reuters.com, 29 August 2014.
33. Camille Hurard and Laurent Huault, '1.2 Million More Vacant Homes in France since 1990, Particularly in Declining Population Areas', insee.fr, 16 January 2024.
34. Pablo Hernández de Cos, 'The Spanish Housing Market', Banco de España, 29 April 2024.
35. Instituto Nacional de Estadística, 'Population and Housing Censuses 2021 – Results on Households and Dwellings', ine.es, 30 June 2023.
36. Nikos Roussanoglou, 'Short Supply Lifts House Prices', ekathimerini .com, 1 February 2024.
37. Nikos Roussanoglou, 'Opening 700,000 Vacant Houses Could be a Gamechanger', ekathimerini.com, 9 January 2024.
38. Statista, 'Total Number and per Capita Number of Housing Starts in Italy 2015–2023', statista.com, 1 August 2024.
39. ANSA, 'Almost 1 in 3 Houses in Italy is Unoccupied Says Istat', ansa.it, 1 August 2024.
40. Guy Grainger, 'To Create Net-zero Cities, We Need to Look Hard at Our Older Buildings', weforum.org, 8 November 2022.
41. Statista, 'Distribution of Steel Use Worldwide in 2023, by Industry', statista.com, 26 March 2024.
42. Reports and Data, 'Aluminum Market 2024 – Global Insights, Growth, Trends & Forecast', reportsanddata.com, June 2022.

43. J. Zhou and X. Chen, 'Assessment of Water Consumption During Production of Material and Energy Carriers in China', *Sustainable Production and Consumption*, vol. 20, 2019, 331–41.
44. Jean-Pascal Tricoire, 'Why Buildings Are the Foundation of an Energy-efficient Future', weforum.org, 22 February 2021.
45. Daniel Marsh and David Green, *Air Quality and Emissions in Construction*, urbanhealth.org.uk, September 2022.
46. Kristin Guzder, 'Pollution from Construction: What Are the Types & How Can We Prevent It?', highspeedtraining.co.uk, 29 November 2019.
47. Nick Bano, *Against Landlords: How to Solve the Housing Crisis*, London: Verso, 2024, 2.
48. House of Commons Library, 'Industries in the UK', commons library.parliament.uk, 3 October 2024.
49. Ibid., 5.

11. What's Done Is Done

1. Rolf J. Goebel, 'Berlin's Architectural Citations: Reconstruction, Simulation, and the Problem of Historical Authenticity', *PMLA*, Modern Language Association of America, 2003, 1274.
2. Placemaking is an illegitimate term. See Reinier de Graaf, *architect, verb.: The New Language of Building*, London: Verso, 2023.
3. 'Het Palast der Republik', *Andere Tijden*, 9 November 2004.
4. See also Chapter 10.
5. Oliver Wainwright, '"Sometimes the answer is to do nothing": unflashy French duo take architecture's top prize', theguardian.com, 16 March 2021.
6. Catherine Slessor, 'Grand Parc, Bordeaux Review – A Rush of Light, Air and Views', theguardian.com, 12 May 2019.

7. Fundació Mies van der Rohe, 'De Flat Kleiburg Wins the European Union Prize for Contemporary Architecture – Mies van der Rohe Award 2017', miesbcn.com, 12 May 2017.
8. Antonio Gómez-Palacio, 'Deep Retrofits: How Repurposing Old Buildings Can Mitigate Climate Change', *World Economic Forum*, 7 February 2024.
9. Haworth Tompkins, 'National Theatre', *AJ Buildings Library*, 2015.
10. Gardiner & Theobald, 'Tender Price Indicator Q4 2022', *Gardiner & Theobald Market Intelligence*, October 2022.
11. Reuters, 'France Plans New Measures to Tackle Housebuilding Slump', reuters.com, 29 August 2014.
12. Jorge Cristóbal García et al., *Techno-economic and Environmental Assessment of Construction and Demolition Waste Management in the European Union*, European Commission: Joint Research Centre, January 2024.
13. NL Times, 'Sustainability Measures Threatening Thousands of Pre-War Buildings in the Netherlands', nltimes.nl, 1 November 2023.
14. Statista, 'Total Number and Per Capita Number of Housing Starts in Italy 2015–2023', statista.com, 1 August 2024.
15. Cristóbal García et al., *Techno-economic and Environmental Assessment*.
16. Homes England, 'Fact Sheet 1: The Need for Homes', gov.uk, 16 January 2024.
17. Will Hurst, 'Demolishing 50,000 Buildings a Year Is a National Disgrace', thetimes.com, 28 June 2021.
18. Homes for Scotland, 'Existing Housing Need in Scotland', homesforscotland.com, 7 March 2023.
19. Phineas Harper, 'Britain Is Addicted to the Wrecking Ball. It's Trashing Our Heritage and the Planet', theguardian.com, 10 February 2023.

20. John Campbell, 'Republic of Ireland "Needs 35,000 New Homes a Year"', bbc.co.uk, 2 July 2024.
21. Cristóbal García et al., *Techno-economic and Environmental Assessment.*
22. Mary K. Jacob, 'There's a Whopping 7.2M Home Shortage in the US Housing Market', nypost.com, 28 February 2024.
23. Resource Central, 'Deconstruction vs Demolition', resource central.org, 24 March 2023.
24. 'Protestation des artistes contre la tour de M. Eiffel', *Le Temps*, 14 February 1887.
25. UNESCO, 'About Us: History and Mission', unesdoc.unesco.org, 1945.
26. ICOMOS, *The Venice Charter (1964) for the Conservation and Restoration of Monuments and Sites*, article 5.

12. Unlearn Vitruvius

1. Le Corbusier, *Creation Is a Patient Search*, New York: Frederick A. Praeger, 1960.
2. Eddie Arruza, 'The Battle over Goldberg's Prentice Women's Hospital', news.wttw.com, 7 August 2012.
3. John Ruskin, *The Seven Lamps of Architecture*, London: Smith, Elder & Co., 1849, 233.
4. Eames Foundation, 'The 250 Year Project', eamesfoundation.org, 2023.
5. Barnabas Calder and Florian Urban, 'It Is Time No Longer to Praise the Seagram Building but to Bury It', *The Architects' Journal*, 10 November 2022.
6. Vitruvius, *The Ten Books on Architecture*, Cambridge: Harvard University Press, 1914, Book I, Chapter III, 17.
7. Jean Prouvé, quoted in Christian Enjolras, *Jean Prouvé. Les maisons de Meudon 1949–1999*, Paris : Éditions de la Villette, 2003.
8. R. Buckminster Fuller, *Nine Chains to the Moon*, Carbondale: Southern Illinois University Press, 1963, 329.

9. Donald Trump, interview with Bloomberg, Economic Club of Chicago, youtube.com, 15 October 2024.

13. Forget Sustainability

1. Lauren Sommer, 'Here's How Far Behind the World Is on Reining in Climate Change', npr.org, 27 October 2022.
2. Barack Obama, 'Statement by the President on the Paris Climate Agreement', obamawhitehouse.archives.gov, 12 December 2015.
3. Frans Timmermans, 'Speech by Executive Vice-President Timmermans at the Parliament Plenary on the outcome of COP26 in Glasgow', ec.europa.eu, 24 November 2021.
4. Boris Johnson, 'PM Press Conference Statement at the G20: 31 October 2021', gov.uk, 31 October 2021.
5. Michael D. Shear, 'Trump Will Withdraw U.S. From Paris Climate Agreement', nytimes.com, 1 June 2017.
6. Nectar Gan, 'Xi Says China Will Follow its Own Carbon Reduction Path as US Climate Envoy Kerry Meets Top Officials in Beijing', cnn.com, 19 July 2023.
7. United Nations Environment Programme, *2022 Global Status Report for Buildings and Construction*, unep.org, 2022.
8. Hassell Studio, 'Lunar Master Plan: Moon Base for the European Space Agency', hassellstudio.com, January 2024.
9. Foster + Partners, 'Mars Habitat', fosterandpartners.com, 2015.
10. Bjarke Ingels Group, 'Mars Science City', big.dk, 2017.
11. Ernest Becker, *The Denial of Death*, New York: Free Press, 1973.
12. R. Buckminster Fuller, *Operating Manual for Spaceship Earth*, Carbondale: Southern Illinois University Press, 1969.
13. Rem Koolhaas and Bruce Mau, 'Whatever Happened to Urbanism?', in *S,M,L,XL*, New York: The Monacelli Press, 1995.
14. Antonio Sant'Elia, 'Manifesto of Futurist Architecture', italian futurism.org, 1914.

15. Archigram, *Archigram Magazine*, no. 8, 1968.
16. Water Technology, 'Delta Works Flood Protection Project, Netherlands', water-technology.net.
17. NL Times, 'Netherlands Needs up to €33 Billion to Shore up Flood Defenses; Far More than Estimates', nltimes.nl, 8 November 2023.

14. On Whose Terms?

1. A fictionalized account of the relation between Gian Lorenzo Bernini and Louis XIV, based on Jeanne Morgan Zarucchi, 'Bernini and Louis XIV: A Duel of Egos', *Notes in the History of Art*, vol. 25, no. 2, 2006, 32–8.
2. Tom Wolfe, *From Bauhaus to Our House*, New York: Farrar, Straus and Giroux, 1981.
3. Human Rights Watch, '"The Island of Happiness": Exploitation of Migrant Workers on Saadiyat Island, Abu Dhabi', hrw.org, 19 May 2009.
4. Jean Nouvel, quoted in Kim Willsher, 'Architect Defends Treatment of Workers at Louvre Abu Dhabi', theguardian.com, 24 September 2017.
5. Foster + Partners, quoted in Helen Gilbert, 'Poor Working Conditions Continue for Starchitect Projects in Abu Dhabi', architectsjournal.co.uk, 12 May 2014.
6. Zaha Hadid, quoted in James Riach, 'Zaha Hadid Defends Qatar World Cup Role Following Migrant Worker Deaths', theguardian.com, 25 February 2014.
7. Foster + Partners, quoted in Gilbert, 'Poor Working Conditions Continue for Starchitect Projects in Abu Dhabi'.
8. The White House, 'Promoting Beautiful Federal Civic Architecture', whitehouse.gov, 20 January 2025.

9. Economist Intelligence Unit, 'Democracy Index 2023: Age of Conflict', economist.com, 2024.

Conclusion

1. Jillian Ambrose, 'ExxonMobil and Chevron Suffer Shareholder Rebellions over Climate', theguardian.com, 26 May 2021.